THE END OF PUNISHMENT

THE END
OF PUNISHMENT

CHRISTIAN PERSPECTIVES
ON THE CRISIS
IN CRIMINAL JUSTICE

Chris Wood

with Foreword by
Rev. Professor Duncan B. Forrester

and Preface by
Dr David Garland

PUBLISHED ON BEHALF OF
The CENTRE for
THEOLOGY and PUBLIC ISSUES
UNIVERSITY of EDINBURGH
BY
SAINT ANDREW PRESS
EDINBURGH

First published in 1991 by
SAINT ANDREW PRESS
121 George Street, Edinburgh EH2 4YN
on behalf of
The CENTRE for THEOLOGY and PUBLIC ISSUES
UNIVERSITY of EDINBURGH

Copyright © 1991 The Centre for Theology and Public Issues,
University of Edinburgh

ISBN 0 86153 145 0

British Library of Cataloguing in Publication Data
A catalogue record of this book
is available from the British Library

ISBN 0-86153-145-0

This book is set in 11/12 pt Times Roman

Printed and Bound by Bell and Bain Ltd., Glasgow

Contents

Part 3 ACTION

Foreword

This book is the fruit of a study project on Principles and Assumptions of Penal Policy started in 1988 by the Centre for Theology and Public Issues at Edinburgh University. This study was initiated following a Conference on "Law and Order: Prospects for the Future" which the Centre organised in late 1986. The Conference suggested powerfully that the British penal system was in a state of crisis, uncertain about values and principles, and confused about what the system was for and what it was intended to achieve. The Conference heard from a range of people about the damage this uncertainty caused, especially when compounded by the fact that society loaded so many incompatible expectations on the system, and then denied it the resources to fulfill any of them in an adequate and humane way, leading to a quite disgraceful overloading of the system.

All this suggested that underlying the penal crisis were quite fundamental issues of values and of theology — uncertainties about how to understand and treat human beings, about the nature of society, about sin, and offence, forgiveness and reconciliation. Quite clearly these were matters that theologians should address, and could only address adequately in collaboration with others. We attempted to build on two earlier endeavours along these lines: *The Coming Penal Crisis*, edited by Tony Bottoms and Ronald Preston (Edinburgh, Scottish Academic Press, 1980) which reported on an important conference of criminologists and theologians; and Adrian Speller's *Breaking Out* (London, Hodder and Stoughton, 1986), which was the result of the work of a group organised by the British Council of Churches.

By 1988 it was clear that the penal crisis was on us in no

uncertain terms. Prison riots were simply the most obvious symptom of a deep uncertainty about what the penal system is *for*: growing disenchantment with rehabilitation as the primary purpose of prisons led either to a strange vacuum in penal policy, or the replacement of rehabilitation with practices based on often ill-defined understandings of a "justice model" of punishment, which at their worst made prisons no more than human warehouses. The effect of this confusion on many people operating the system has been serious, but there has also been (as we know from our dealings with the Scottish Prison Service in recent years) a deep commitment to the reform and renewal of the system.

We therefore felt the time was ripe and the need was urgent to establish a Working Group to examine some of these issues in a serious fashion, with special attention to underlying assumptions, principles and conflicts, and with a special eye to the possibility of constructive insights coming from the Christian theological tradition. As in the other studies undertaken by the Centre, the Group represented a very wide range of experience and of discipline, and we had a special concern to attend to the powerless, in this case particularly prisoners and the victims of crime. As we examined a diversity of experience, we discovered, to our surprise, that many people struggling to work in a human way within the system have such frustrations and unease that they too must count as oppressed. A prominent prison governor said at one of our conferences that he often felt that he should apologise to the prisoners for the conditions in which he was obliged to keep them.

The Working Group met regularly over a two year period, mainly to discuss working papers prepared by members of the group. We had two residential weekends. A subgroup took special responsibility for drafting and revising the theological material used by the Group. We visited five Scottish prisons and had extended discussions with prisoners and staff. The Scottish Prison Service laid on an illuminating seminar on recent developments in penal policy in Scotland at their headquarters in Edinburgh. A wide range of organisations and individuals gave us written or verbal submissions, and many spent a hard working day with us considering early drafts for the book. In 1990 we held a Day Conference at which Terence Morris, Anthony Duff, Ronald Preston, and Tony Bottoms gave papers relating to the principal themes of the Group's work. These have now been published as *Justice, Guilt, and Forgiveness in the Penal System* (Centre for Theology and Public Issues Occasional Paper No. 18), and a number of references to these are contained within the text that follows. In addition to acknowledging the contribution of these authors, we wish to extend our appreciation also to a number of people, some of whose ideas, comments, writing, and illustrations have been used, in particular Professor Derek McClintock, Sheriffs Douglas Allan and Nigel Thomson, the late Andrew Meikle, Sue Moodie, David Croft, David Rowbotham, Robert MacKay, Roy Kilner, and George Moore.

The Group's discussions started, possibly predictably, with examining the major theories of punishment. At this stage of the Group's work, two things started to happen. First, we discovered that none of these theories, or even all of them together, explained much of what was happening in the penal system. From this we went on to conclude that theories, for all their importance, can also conceal much that is important, or even lend a subtle veneer of justification to practices which are in fact intolerable. Second, the theologians in the group resisted the request from some of the other members to put "the Christian theology of punishment" alongside the other theories. That, it was argued, is not a proper understanding of theology, nor was it yet time at that stage to start talking theologically. Theology came later, *after* we had embarked on experience.

Theology emerged first in a fragmentary way — clues, hints, and hunches, derived from the Christian tradition, which we began to use as a way of interpreting experience and criticizing theory and policy. To give a crucial example: a member of the group said, almost as an aside, that the two themes that were hardly ever mentioned in the penal system were *guilt* and *forgiveness*. These, and similar themes, increasingly shaped the discussion of the Group, and indeed, our overall conclusion, reflected in the eventual title of the book, ie *that a system of punishment can only be justified if it is directed towards forgiveness and reconciliation.*

Coming from such diverse backgrounds, we all felt that we were wrestling with rather unusual questions, and handling them in a way which was different from that common in our various disciplines and professions. I think all of us learned a lot and were deeply challenged by the experience of the Group. We all became increasingly concerned about much that is happening in the British penal system, not just to prisoners and victims of crime, but to people of humanity and vocation working within the system, and perhaps even to society itself. Along with horror at some of the things done in the name of a civilized society, went also excitement at the increasing awareness that there is today a widespread determination to seek for radical reform and humanisation of the system. To that we hope this book will make some small contribution.

In particular we hope that this book may do a little to encourage society to face its responsibility for what is done in its name; that those who make policy and work within the system may find it supportive, suggestive and encouraging; and that Christians and churches may see more clearly that they have insights, responsibilities, and values which are important for a humane penal system in a decent society.

The Centre is grateful to Chris Wood for his hard and effective work in writing up the Group's deliberations; to the West London Mission of the Methodist Church which encouraged him to take on this task and allowed him the time to do so; and to the Trust whose generosity made this study possible.

DUNCAN B. FORRESTER

Members of the Group

(in alphabetical order)

Dr. John Basson	Forensic Psychiatrist
Philip Brodie, Q.C.	Advocate
Martha Bruce	Retired Prison Governor
Rev. Claus Clausen	Community Minister
Rev. Prof. Duncan Forrester	Professor of Christian Ethics, and Director of the Centre for Theology and Public Issues
Dr. David Garland	Reader in Criminology
Rev. Charlotte Henderson	Prison Chaplain
Charles Hills	Retired Prison Governor and Member of the Parole Board
Dr. Robert McCreadie	Lecturer in Scots Law
Rev. Alastair MacGregor	Parish Minister and Queen's Counsel
Alastair MacKinnon	Research Student
Rev. James Nelson	Parish Minister, and Life Sentence Prisoner
Rev. Willy Slavin	Prison Chaplain
Rev. James Wilkie	Parish Minister, and former Director Youth Treatment Centre
Chris Wood	Social Worker

Preface

The End of Punishment appears at an important moment in British penal history. After decades of delay and inaction, it now looks as if the necessary political will may exist to address the long-term problems of criminal justice and to bring about a much-needed restructuring of its institutions. The Woolf Report, which followed the massive prison disturbances of April 1990, recommends a series of reforms which, if implemented, would transform the fabric of Britain's prison system. A Royal Commission — the first for a dozen years — has recently been announced to investigate the whole process of criminal procedure. A series of Green and White Papers has proposed new ways of dealing with offenders which rely less upon custody and more upon community-based measures. The Scottish Prison Service has published a series of discussion documents which reconsider the objectives of imprisonment and sketch out new proposals which promise to introduce standards of justice and care into institutions where these have all too often been lacking. Government ministers have publicly acknowledged that our current practices of punishment are in many respects insupportable and have shown themselves to be willing to consider serious alternatives. More generally, there is a growing realisation on the part of the public that our system for dealing with offenders is inefficient, out of step with the best practice of our European neighbours, and, above all, has become an undeniable affront to the values of justice, humanity, and decency. Events may turn out differently, and penal reform may once more fade from the political agenda, but it seems at least possible that the 1990s will prove to be a defining moment in the reordering of criminal justice. The objective of this book is to seize that opportunity and to open up these important issues for discussion by the widest possible audience.

In such a context, the character of this book is a significant one. It is not the product of criminological academics, or policy experts, or of insiders whose job it is to run the system, but rather of a disparate group of people, some with limited expertise, some with none at all, who have had to struggle to develop a general understanding of a rather bewildering and complex process and to think through, slowly and painfully, the tangled moral issues which underlie it. This in itself is an important achievement. The modern organisation of social life is such that deep and disturbing problems such as the punishment of offenders tend to be put "behind the scenes" — defined as the task of specialised institutions on the margins of society and delegated to professionals who can be trusted to relieve us of the need to confront or even to think about the issues involved. In this way, punishment becomes a routine technical task for paid officials, rather than a profound moral and social problem with which all of us, as members of society, should be concerned. Such an arrangement has, of course, obvious and important advantages: it protects offenders from volatile swings of public opinion, it renders their treatment unemotive, bureaucratic, professional, and of course it relieves the rest of us — most of the time — of the need to worry about the fate of those involved.

But putting the problem out of sight in this way does not make it disappear — as prison disturbances forcibly remind us — and the delegation of tasks to professionals does not make the definition of those tasks any less the responsibility of the society in whose name they are carried out. Moreover, the one hidden cost of this arrangement is that the public can become seriously uninformed about the real facts of crime and its punishment, and in such circumstances may be easily and disproportionately influenced by emotive political appeals or by the sensational headlines which accompany particularly heinous cases. Instead of providing penal practitioners with a clear and authoritative remit, "the public" too frequently allows itself to appear as a reactionary obstacle to sensible and humane practice.

The present book represents an attempt to overcome the modern division between penal professionals and the public whom they serve. It seeks to address important penal issues in a manner which can readily be understood by the lay person. It seeks to bring back into focus the fact that penal institutions house individual men and women, not faceless offenders and officers, and to remind readers that the fate of these people is our collective responsibility. And in trying to come to terms with the human problems which are endemic in our penal institutions, it seeks to enlist the concern, the support, and the active participation of a broader cross-section of people than is currently involved.

The initiative which led to the production of this work occurred under the auspices of a Christian theological institution. This fact strikes me as particularly apposite considering the long history of the Christian Churches' involvement in penal issues, although from our contemporary standpoint the record of that involvement is by no means unambiguous. Religious faiths and theological doctrines lay behind many of the most important penal innovations of the last few centuries, notably the early penitentiary prisons and the systems of prison visiting, after-care, and probation which emerged in the prison's wake. Similarly the evangelical concerns with reformation and with the regenerative capabilities of all men and women, however sinful, was an important element underpinning the rise of the rehabilitative ideal and the various correctional practices associated with it.

But such are the ambivalences of punishment — and indeed the ambivalences of the Christian faith — that each of these measures came in time to reveal aspects of themselves which were more repressive, and less morally defensible than had originally been apparent. Consequently, the Churches now seem to be implicated not in a story of reform and improvement, but instead in a less attractive narrative in which the apparatuses of discipline become ever more inconsistent and the procedures of exclusion and condemnation ever more unforgiving.

This long and repeated experience of apparently humane reforms which later reveal elements of cruelty and inhumanity should make us cautious about our proposals for change. It should lead us to scrutinise penal measures for their hidden aspects, to scrutinise our own attitudes for their hidden motivations, and to treat even our most certain knowledge, intuition and belief as being always provisional and open to challenge. Above all it should lead us to pay close and respectful attention to the experiences of those who undergo the pains of our punishments and who know what it is that they involve.

The practice of the working group has tried to absorb these lessons, and has interpreted the Christian tradition in a reflexive, non-dogmatic way. Drawing upon the theological understandings of some of its members, the group has identified a number of issues which, it felt, might form a bridge between the traditional concerns of Christian theology and the practical problems of criminal justice. "Justice" was one primary and essential theme. In the penal realm, at different times and places, various conceptions of justice have been stressed, sometimes emphasising the equal consideration and due process of "formal justice", some-times the more substantive justice involved in individualised treatments or rehabilitative policies. Moreover, as critics have always pointed out, the ideals of penal justice are, to some extent, dependent for their realisation upon the prior achievement of some measure of social justice. Justice in punishment is thus a problematic ideal which raises, in an acute and concrete form, many of the questions traditionally addressed by Christian theology. The potential contribution of the Christian conceptions of justine was thus an obvious starting place.

Similarly, concepts such as "guilt" and "forgiveness" seemed to have a place both in penal policy and in Christian morality, although it quickly became apparent that, in actual fact, both of these terms are rather marginal to the daily practices and concerns of criminal institutions. Legal "guilt" is by no means the same as the personal experience of guilt, and while our penal institutions are geared to deal with those convicted of crimes, it seems clear that they are not adapted to addressing or dealing with guilt in the more profound sense. Nor is it clear that "guilt" should always and wholly be the attribute of the individual offender, leaving the rest of the community uninvolved and not responsible for the conduct of its citizens.

As for "forgiveness", the group soon realised that while modern society is well equipped to express condemnation and to enforce exclusion through institutions designed for these purposes, there is little time or money spent on the process of reconciling or resettling offenders, and virtually no institutional embodiment of the basic Christian value of forgiveness. To think in terms not just of punishment, but also of the end of punishment — of forgiveness — is thus to open up a radical and perhaps a disturbing set of issues for modern penal policy.

The final bridging concept which seemed to link penal issues to theological ones is the notion of "vocation". It is still the case today that many of the people who enter upon a career of working with offenders do so with some sense of moral mission or purpose, even though the penological evangelicism so common in the nineteenth century has largely been displaced by the more professional orientation of the twentieth. It is, however, immensely difficult to sustain this sense of vocation in the face of the practical difficulties and disappointments which are so frequently encountered in dealing with offenders, particularly when so many penal institutions are so deeply demoralised, and at a time when the moral purposes of punishment are subject to much doubt and uncertainty. The problem of vocation in a secular, pluralistic society is one which modern theologians have had to address in their own lives and work, and so, potentially at least, it is an area where the theological and the penological might usefully be brought together.

The arguments and insights which result from this encounter make *The End of Punishment* a trenchant and provocative discussion of what is wrong with our penal system and of how it might be transformed. It is a book which should engage anyone who is disturbed by the scandal of criminal justice and who is willing to rethink the old punitive attitudes which, like the crumbling fabric of our Victorian Prisons, have become a part of the problem that they were intended to solve.

DAVID GARLAND

Author's Preface

I was delighted to receive Duncan Forrester's invitation to join a group of people who were concerned about the vacuum of values in the penal system and who wanted to explore what Christian belief might contribute to the debate about what might replace the "rehabilitative ideal". I had joined the probation service in England and Wales as a direct consequence of my own religious beliefs. There had seemed to be a good "fit" between Christian values and the prevailing views about what the system should be trying to do. I moved to Scotland in part because the arrangements introduced by the Social Work (Scotland) Act emphasised even more the community's responsibility for helping and assisting people in its midst who were in trouble — of whatever kind, including offending.

The temper of the times changed dramatically during the eighties. Social work with offenders was affected by the reductions in public expenditure that affected local authorities. The parole system came under increasing attack, from academics, from politicians, and from prisoners. The very existence of "society" was questioned by those in high places. The boundaries of who was "deserving" of help were defined increasingly tightly. Punishment became an increasing emphasis in policy discussion, and the "justice" model was all the rage.

The goal posts were moved in my own field — probation work — as in that of others in the group. I had been attracted to the idea that probation was there "instead of a sentence": now it was to be emphasised as a punishment, and much less was heard about its essential tasks of advising, assisting, and befriending. Probation had seemed to me to contain a "spark of the divine", in that Christian belief suggested to me that God's response to our wrong-doing was not to inflict punishment, but to offer a chance of new relationship instead.

So I had expected possibly to contribute a paper on probation to the group's work. What I had not bargained for was that the group should entrust me with writing up the whole of its work as a book. That was only possible by virtue of financial assistance from an anonymous trust, and because my present employers, the West London Mission of the Methodist Church, allowed me to undertake the work as part of my ordinary duties. The book seeks to be faithful to the views and work of the group, but any errors or inaccuracies in the text are my responsibility.

Social/probation work with offenders was largely begun by church missionaries. Part of my more recent move to work for the church arose from a concern to reaffirm the relevance of Christian values in the context of dealing with offenders. I hope this book will contribute to that re-affirmation.

CHRIS WOOD

Introduction
Why "The End of Punishment"?

Crime — punishment. It seems a natural association of ideas. The criminal justice system is there to impose punishment on those who are found to have committed crimes. That punishment is supposed variously to achieve retribution, deterrence, prevention, denunciation, rehabilitation — or a mixture of these, even all of them. Punishment is to give people their "just deserts", it is often said. That all feels very acceptable and comfortable.

Perhaps it is unfair of us to disturb this simple scenario. However, one or two important points need to be made by way of opening remarks.

The first is that present arrangements aren't very successful at preventing crime or deterring people from offending, or rehabilitating them. A Home Office document says: "the almost invariable conclusion of the large amount of research that has been undertaken is that *it is hard to show that any one type of sentence is more likely than any other to reduce the likelihood of re-offending, which is high for all*" (quoted in Nicholson, 1986, pp. 41–2). The whole operation of putting people before courts and punishing them may have little influence on the prevention and commission of crime. There is therefore a fundamental question mark over any idea that the answer to the problem of crime lies in the criminal justice system. If it is not the solution to the problem, then there is a further fundamental question as to what it should do and how it should deal with people.

The second point is that in achieving this failure, there is a gross over-reliance on the use of imprisonment. Scotland is *top of an unenviable league* in Western Europe concerning the proportion of the population that gets sent to prison (see, for example, Kinsey, 1986, p. 66). In 1988 the United

Kingdom average figure was 98 per 100,000 population: the figure for Scotland in the same year was 106. This compares with France 92; Germany 86; Sweden 61; and the Netherlands 36. In Scotland this high level of use of imprisonment, albeit with some fluctuations, has been the situation for at least 10 years. Even though the numbers have come down a little, the proportion of people serving longer sentences (over 18 months) has risen markedly.

It is not as if all this use of imprisonment has had much effect on crime rates. Other countries manage with lower levels of use of imprisonment — very significantly so in the case of the Netherlands, which does not have less crime to deal with (see Downes, 1988). There is *no compulsion* to use prison to the extent that we do. It is also very expensive, leaving aside any arguments about morality, or considerations of prison conditions.

Many people have become concerned about the enormous expense this level of use of imprisonment creates. So the idea being advanced now is to make greater use of things like community service and probation, which are cheaper. But in order to do this, we are told, these orders have to be made much "tougher". They have to include "curfews" and "tagging" before anyone, whether judges or public, will "buy" the idea. The phrase of the moment is "punishment in the community" (see Home Office, 1988, and 1989).

For much of this century, pride of place among the aims of punishment has been given to the objective of "rehabilitation" — the idea that offenders (or some of them) could be turned into good citizens. However, the theories underpinning that idea are now discredited and the approach's results do not seem to be any more "successful" than any other. The notion became associated with the "Treatment Model", and it is the theories and outcomes of this particular aspect that have been heavily criticised. However, the whole notion seems to have fallen from grace, along with the values and ideals on which it was initially based. The ideal did, however, give a real sense of purpose to many people working in the system. It gave a feeling that something good could be achieved, both for the individual and for society. It made the idea of punishment more acceptable and live-able with. But now, with the collapse of the ideal and the thought system around it, *we are in a vacuum*. Trying to rehabilitate the ideal of rehabilitation does not seem to be an adequate response to the situation.

"Imprisonment is a practice without a policy" declared a British Council of Churches report in 1986 (Speller, 1986, p. 83) "There is confusion and pessimism about the traditional objectives of retribution, prevention, deterrence, and rehabilitation", wrote the author. "Each has been called into question on practical and moral grounds. What should be firm foundations are looking increasingly unsteady".

Even more recently (1990), and in even stronger terms, a leading criminologist evaluating the use of prison in the Western world wrote, "the theories of individual prevention — rehabilitation, incapacitation, individual deterrence — are unable to defend the prison. Neither is the other major theory of social defence — the theory of general prevention. And neither, finally, is the theory of justice. The prison does not have a defence, *the prison is a fiasco in terms of its own purposes"* (Mathiesen, 1990, p. 19).

One reason for having a system is to prevent "mob justice", and to bring cooler heads to the business of deciding and administering punishment. But woe betide the judge or prison governor who strays too far from what it is thought public opinion may find acceptable. But how is public opinion about crime and criminals formed?

Certain sections of the media encourage a view of criminals as inhuman, as monsters, or animals. Criminals do not have horns or forked tails. There is a "demonology" of criminals. Crime stories feature sex and violence to the extent that people come to believe all crime is of that nature. A majority of people in the country are said to want hanging to be re-introduced; or to want physical punishments and hard labour to be typical penalties. There is a whole industry and activity devoted to maintaining certain stereotypes and pictures of criminals, and to re-inforcing vengeful and vindictive emotions towards them. Whose needs are being met by this?

This does not help people working in the system to have a clear sense of purpose about what they are doing. People working in the system share the natural responses of anger and dismay at the phenomenon of crime. They are confronted with people who have actually committed these kinds of crimes much more frequently and directly than a typical person in the street or pew. People working in the system are doing so on behalf of society, yet can feel at odds with the emphasis on punishment, all that is currently being offered by that society. They expect to represent society and its standards to those with whom they are involved, but may feel out of sympathy with the tenor of that society.

The first message to feed back would be this: *Simply being an agent of society's vengeance and/or punitiveness is not the reason* people work within the system. A system that was dedicated solely to expressing, on society's behalf, feelings of punitiveness and condemnation, would be very unhealthy. Some other purpose and aim are needed if we are not all to be brutalised and dehumanised.

The punishments used most frequently involve little if any meeting or relationship with those who commit crime. Either their money is taken away (fines and compensation), or their liberty (imprisonment). It is as if society does not want to know them. They are put as far away, both literally and metaphorically, as possible. The problem is rejected rather than dealt with.

Many people come to work in the system as a result of personal beliefs and motivations, and want to achieve various aims and objectives, but they feel that they lack any real support from their various "constituencies" or sending communities. That can even be the case for chaplains, who are working in the system very expressly as representatives of the church. They can feel that people in the pew could be surprised if they knew what they were doing and trying to achieve in their ministry.

In the first part of the book we will introduce some of the people in the system, including prisoners, and describe their typical experiences, many of them exceedingly frustrating ones. In part two, we reflect on this experience in the light of theology and Christian faith. And in part three, we explore what kinds of ideas for action result from our reflection on experience.

Part 1

EXPERIENCE

Setting the Scene
and Dramatis Personae

The term "criminal justice system" suggests a single, even homogeneous, entity. In fact the system is made up of a number of parts or sub-systems. Each has its own ways of working, form of organisation, and culture. Whilst many people who are on its receiving end feel that the system is trying to "do them down", as it were, any such conspiracy is not necessarily an actively organised or planned one. The system does not always pull together. There can be competing elements, approaches, and ways of working within it.

There are a number of participants. Each may have a different role, value system, and set of concerns. This short section introduces them briefly, and outlines the different parts of the system.

You, the reader. From the preface above, you may have identified yourself as belonging to one or more of the "audiences" to whom this book is addressed. That suggests you can sit back and watch a play or read a story in which you are not very directly involved. In fact the action goes on in your name. You may become directly involved in its workings, for example as a juror, or as a witness to a crime, or as a victim of a crime. One of our aims is to make you feel more informed about, and even involved in, what goes on — and that you may want to change it.

The Victim has very little role to play in the system as it works at present. It may be to give evidence in a court case, and to be cross-examined about it. There are few, if any, ways in which the victim's views and experiences are taken into account by the system. Often victims hear nothing after the event about what happened, whether anyone was arrested and/or prosecuted, what happened to them, who they were, and so on. There is some evidence that what may appear to be a minor crime can have quite disproportional consequences for the victim. While there are statutory services in relation to offenders (for example, probation), what caring services exist specifically for victims do so because voluntary societies have been set up for the purpose.

The Police investigate crime and report their findings to the prosecution service (the Procurator Fiscal in Scotland, or the recently established Crown Prosecution Service in England and Wales). Whilst the Police will have views and opinions about the offence and about what should happen to the offender, the decision about prosecution and what follows is not necessarily theirs. Their role is to provide evidence and information, and to give it in court if necessary. They also have some areas of choice, in deciding whether to record a crime, or to deal with it by other methods which do not bring the person further into the criminal justice system.

The Prosecutor has two main questions to consider. The first is whether there is enough evidence to prosecute. The second is, even if there is enough evidence, whether or not to prosecute. Nowadays more thought is being given to whether, in all cases, prosecution should be automatic.

More use has been made of warnings of various kinds. Concepts of "diversion" (as it has become known) have become familiar in the sphere of juvenile justice; in Scotland the whole *system* for dealing with juveniles who commit offences (The Children's Hearing System) is a diversionary one by definition, in that — on the whole — children in trouble are not dealt with by a criminal court at all. In some areas of England and Wales, the use of cautioning and other diversionary strategies has reduced the number of children appearing before courts and going to custody.

The adoption of diversionary ideas in relation to *adults* is a relatively new phenomenon. Scottish Procurators Fiscal have been developing arrangements whereby some adult offenders are "diverted" directly to social work schemes of various kinds instead of going to court, if it is felt that giving help is better than prosecution in some less serious cases. However, there have been debates as to whether in some cases (for example, wife battering) there should not always be a prosecution, because only by this means can the behaviour be denounced and the person confronted with their offending.

The Courts can only deal with those cases that prosecutors put before them. There are various levels of court: in some instances the law may determine which court deals with a case, otherwise the prosecutor may decide in which court to start a case. The first task for the court is to decide whether the person charged is guilty. In serious cases this will involve trial by jury; in lesser cases the judge or magistrate(s) may have to decide guilt themselves. The next task is to impose sentence.

The courts have a limited range of sentences they can impose, though the possibilities have been expanded in recent years. It is often said that sentencing has only become a problem in the last 25 years; before that it was prison, or a fine. The only other alternatives were versions, in effect, of doing nothing — discharging the person, or deferring sentence. The use of probation was initially for juveniles and adolescents: its relevance to older offenders can still need to be emphasised. Community service orders are an invention of the 1970s. The 1970s also saw, in England and Wales, the introduction of the suspended sentence of imprisonment, and later of partially suspended sentences. Any sentence of imprisonment in Scotland has to take immediate effect. In some instances, the law prevents a court from imposing a particular kind of sentence (especially a custodial one) unless it has a report from a social worker/probation officer about the background of the person, and which considers the possible non-custodial options that might be available.

A "duty solicitor" system operates in the Scottish courts for anyone who has been taken into custody by the Police and who may not have a solicitor of their own. There is also a system of legal aid, but concern has been growing at attempts to restrict the availability of legal aid. Financial restrictions on the scheme could result in poorer people being denied access to justice.

The social worker/probation officer has a range of duties and responsibilities. He or she has to provide reports about people to the courts when they are required, and should consider in those reports what non-custodial options might achieve. If the court makes a probation order or a community service order, the social worker/probation officer has to supervise that order. That involves responsibilities to the person under supervision as well as to the court. Social workers and probation officers may also be involved with people who owe fines. They also work within prisons. They have responsibilities for supervising people who are released from prison on various kinds of after-care and parole licence. More generally they have a responsibility for helping all kinds of people in need in the community, part of whose difficulties may include involvement with the criminal justice system.

Psychiatrists may also have to provide reports to courts if there is a question as to the person's sanity, or as to whether they are fit to plead. They may also be involved in providing treatment for people in trouble with the law who are also mentally ill. There are some instances in which people can be detained in mental hospital by order of the court, and the responsibility for their treatment and discharge back into the community may rest with the psychiatrist.

Prisons are not only used for people sentenced to serve time in them by a court, but in two other very significant ways as well.

They are used to hold people "on remand" awaiting trial and/or sentence. Although the law presumes that someone is innocent until they are proved guilty, very substantial numbers of people are held in prison until the court can hear their case. Conditions for remand prisoners are often amongst the worst in the system, and have been repeatedly condemned, even by official people responsible for the system. In spite of legislation aimed at promoting the use of bail, a considerable number of exceptions to the presumption in favour of bail are found by the courts. The use of bail hostels has been suggested, but few, if any, exist in Scotland. Scotland has a "110 day rule" which limits the time that a person can be held in custody before trial. However many people detained in custody before their trial are either acquitted, or, if found guilty, do not receive a custodial sentence.

Prisons are also used for people who do not pay fines. Most people who are fined do pay, but in recent years there has been a noticeable increase in the number of people, and particularly young people, being sent to prison for not paying their fines. The problem seems to be acute in Scotland, but is far from negligible in England and Wales. Often the amounts owed are relatively small. Equally importantly, the original offence and circumstances were such that the court did not intend that prison should be the consequence. One idea currently under discussion is that of the "day fine", or some other method of making a fine proportional to a person's income.

Being sentenced to prison is "doing time". There is an enormous range of lengths of time that people may have to serve in prison — from a matter of a few weeks up to a "life" sentence. In some cases it has been suggested that "life" should mean that the person will never come out of prison alive. In Scotland the proportion of people serving "short" sentences (less than 18 months) is quite considerable. However at the other end of the scale, the number of people being sentenced to long sentences is increasing.

Parole is a system introduced in 1968 whereby some longer sentence prisoners are chosen for early release into the community under the supervision of a social worker/probation officer. They are regarded while on parole as "serving their sentence in the community". Decisions about who to release are taken under the aegis of a complicated bureaucratic machine that is often faceless to the prisoner. Uncertainty about parole is said by many prisoners to be a great source of tension and anxiety while serving a sentence. Concern about parole has become so great generally in recent years that on both sides of the Border official committees have been set up to review the whole notion and practice of early release from prison.

The organisation of the criminal justice system reflects these different elements within it. Prosecution, courts, and prisons are organised as parts of central government, but are under different departments and ministers. The catchment areas of prisons may be wider than those of courts. Social work services in Scotland are part of local government, whose boundaries may be different again. In Scotland, local councillors, as elected representatives of the local community, have a very direct responsibility for part of the criminal justice system. Services for victims, where they exist, are provided mainly by voluntary organisations created specially for the purpose. They may need to spend a considerable part of their energy in securing funds from both central and local government in order to exist at all.

A central feature of the organisation of the penal system is the principle of the independence of the judiciary. Whilst this is clearly an important constitutional principle, it can create problems if the sentencing part of a judge's role is undertaken in isolation from other concerns of social and penal policy. The management of prisons, and the organisation and workloads of social work and probation services, are utterly dependent on the myriad decisions of individual sentencers across the land dealing with thousands of cases on the basis of passing sentence for this offence, on this day, and relating to that person. Whilst, for example, the Scottish Prison Service is trying to develop a business like and planned approach to the management of its institutions within the criminal justice system, it has to do so on the most tenuous basis of assumptions about what sentencers will do. If those assumptions prove wrong, the carefully nurtured plans can soon require drastic rethinking.

The system is not a homogeneous entity that always works to one end or policy. Any one part may not necessarily agree to, or work along with, the methods and ideas of another. The system may reflect the fact that there are competing

ideas in the wider society as to how to respond to people
who offend.

The Victim

The victim's role in the criminal justice system is very small
indeed. It is largely restricted to reporting the crime to the
police and giving evidence in court if required. There is no
further involvement in prosecution, no consultation about
possible options, and little if any information if a prosecution does ensue. Rarely, until recently, did a court consider
even financial compensation as a matter of course.

Frequently victims are portrayed by the media as vindictive towards offenders and complaining that punishment is
not sufficiently severe. The evidence from wide-ranging
crime surveys, however, paints a rather different picture.
Criminal justice policy might take account of the fact
that people are less primitive towards law breakers than
may be imagined. Asked how "their" offender might be
treated, victims showed awareness and support for court
sentences involving community service and compensation,
and frequently favoured informal warnings and reparations.
The system may therefore be behaving more harshly than
many victims would wish.

"We believe that too much attention is paid to punishment and too little to redressing the wrong done, and that
nothing like enough consideration is given to the victim in
the criminal process", wrote the Hodgson Committee
(1984). Again, assumptions may be made by the system that
victims do not want to be involved, which do not square with
the experiences and wishes of victims. It is rare for victims to
be excessively punitive. Rather they may want to be
involved in decisions about prosecution, and especially they
may want recognition of the trauma they have suffered, even
from relatively "minor" crimes. They may be less punitive
than the system that is punishing at least in part on their
behalf. There is little "fit" between the interests of victims
and the preoccupations and assumptions of the system.

The Second British Crime Survey reported that 49% of

victims said they would be prepared or wanted to meet the offender. It suggested that there was a clear demand amongst victims for some sort of reparation from offenders. The first such survey had suggested that some incidents go unreported because victims judge them too trivial to justify calling the Police.

Reparation is the making of amends by an offender either to his or her own victim ("direct reparation"), or to the victims of other offenders ("indirect reparation"). It may take the form of financial compensation, restitution, atonement, or the performance of some service for the victim. It may also be achieved by means of mediating an agreed settlement between victim and offender, either by face to face meeting or through a go-between, or by the decision of a third party (Home Office, Research and Planning Unit Paper no. 33, 1985).

Yet the workings of the criminal justice system make no allowance for anything other than financial compensation, and even that has been upgraded only recently. Meetings, negotiation, and personal reparation, where they occur, are the exceptions that prove the rule. Experiments are only just beginning.

The criminal justice system is a punishment dominated system. Yet this domination may neither serve the interests of victims, nor even express the true wishes of many of them. The only emphasis currently being introduced is on financial compensation. Bentham wrote, "compensation will answer the purpose of punishment, but punishment will not answer the purpose of compensation. By compensation, therefore, two great ends of justice are both answered at a time, by punishment only one" (Quoted in Hodgson, 1984, p. 6).

At the outset, therefore, we find a criminal justice system that is preoccupied with dealing solely with the offender by punishing him or her. It is by and large a two-party system that leaves out a crucial third party — the victim. It makes assumptions about the wishes and interests of the victim that are not true to the latter's experience. It leaves the victim in great ignorance about the prosecution and sentencing of the offender. It allows them no scope or part in that whole process. It does little to assist them if they do have to play a part, such as giving evidence. Any support and counselling that is provided is given by voluntary organisations and not as a statutory right, whereas offenders may have certain rights to particular levels of support and treatment. Victims are largely excluded by the criminal justice system. They are not seen as integral players in the drama. Their wishes — to be recognised, to understand what happened to them, to maybe meet the offender and to have their feelings understood, to have personal reparation and compensation — seem to be taken no account of by a system which is focussed primarily on the punishment of offenders.

Society generally tends to see the victim as "good" and the offender as "bad", and the two as quite different categories of people. The point can be made, however, that some offenders can also be victims — both literally, in that their homes may be broken into, their property stolen, and so on — and also more metaphorically in that they may be victims of social injustice, deprivation, disadvantage and so on. To confuse the issue even more, there are some circumstances in which it may be a matter of chance as to who is victim and who is offender . . .

Two rival gangs of youths set out one evening, deliberately armed with chains, knives, and other weapons to contest an area of disputed "territory" on a housing estate. At the end of the night, one young man was in a hospital operating theatre, and another in Police custody. The first spent the next ten years in a wheelchair, the second served a sentence of life imprisonment. At first sight, the one in the wheelchair was the victim. Yet both set off that evening with evil, if not murderous, intent. Which ended up where was largely a matter of chance. Whichever way you look at it, two young lives were ruined by that evening's incident. "Labels" can be deceptive.

The Sentencer

When the sentencer does something acceptable — whether for victim, offender, newspaper reader, lawyer, social worker — the individual concerned declares that he or she has got "justice". The fact that each individual in that situation will have different ideas of "justice" probably does not trouble them. But if it goes against that individual's ideas, then the complaint is that "it's a *travesty* of justice." How is the sentencer to please anyone, if that is the case?

What Policy should a Sentencer Adopt?

Society invests sentencers with considerable power and great dignity. It is as if, in the confusion, there have to be some people who appear to be sure of what they are doing. If everyone else has got different ideas about sentencing, are sentencers themselves any clearer about what they are doing?

It would seem not. A standard work on sentencing in Scotland declares, "it is difficult, if not impossible, to discern any clearly intelligible policy for dealing with those who break the law" (Nicholson, The Law and Practice of Sentencing in Scotland, 1981, p. 1). This book, by a serving sheriff (judge in Scotland), is notable in that it sets out not just the law to do with sentences, but also how one person approaches sentencing. On the whole, sentencers have not been encouraged or even allowed to discuss their task with a wider public. Perhaps judges themselves do not want to admit that they may have doubts and uncertainties about sentencing.

At a recent international conference held in Edinburgh, two judges, one from Scotland and one from England, said publicly that it was difficult for persons appointed to the Bench to understand the problems of offenders from deprived areas, and that something needed to be done. "We don't understand what it is like to live in a poor housing scheme with a very high house-breaking rate, with social security, or in a single parent situation. We have great difficulty in comprehending what life is like. There is a large group who don't understand what the criminal law is about, and who regard the police as enemies. We have somehow to get some understanding of what people in these situations are facing" (Glasgow Herald, 7.9.90).

There appears to be something of a lottery in sentencing. The disparity in sentences exceeds what might be accounted for simply by the variety or individuality of different cases. There is evidence of a geographical lottery that is something much more than rumour about your chances before Judge X, or whether Judge Y has had a good lunch. The evidence has to do with the chances of getting bail, or of receiving a custodial sentence, for similar offences, or in comparable circumstances. It shows that these chances can be significantly different in different court areas, and according to racial group.

People expect sentences to deter offenders: and some also hope that prison may reform people. Yet the same official booklet quoted earlier says, "It would be wrong to impose a custodial sentence in a case where that severe penalty was not warranted by the crime in question merely in the hope of achieving a deterrent or reformative effect, which *experience suggests is unlikely to materialise*" (quoted in Nicholson, *Sentencing Policy and the Failure of Rehabilitation*, 1986, pp. 41/2). So, a sentencer who tries to meet public expectations of deterrence, and hopes to do some good along with that, has used prison inappropriately.

So which sentences do "work"? Reviewing the evidence from research, the Home Office official booklet of guidance to sentencers came to the pretty gloomy conclusion noted earlier: "... the almost invariable conclusion of the considerable amount of research which has been undertaken is that it is hard to show that any one type of sentence is more likely than any other to reduce the likelihood of offending, *which is high for all*" (ibid). The short answer seems to be that "nothing works better than anything else".

Problems and Frustrations in Sentencing

If rehabilitation as a general aim of sentencing is now somewhat suspect, it may nonetheless be possible to identify particular instances in which it can be tried. The practical problem is, how, in a crowded court room on a busy day, with the minimal information at a sentencer's disposal, such cases are to be spotted.

Typically, what we grandly call a "criminal justice system" can look more like a conveyor belt. It is hard, when confronted with a list of 30 or more "breaches of the peace" following the previous evening's football match, to do more than hand out a fairly standard fine. The prosecutor simply says something like, "shouting and swearing, M'Lud"; the defence lawyer mouths some platitudes about a new job to start on Monday, and how much they all depend on him at home; and there is a list of maybe one or two previous convictions of a similar kind. It all takes about two minutes.

If the sentencer does want to pause and think — perhaps to ask a direct question to the person in the dock, or to ask the social worker to speak to them for a while downstairs to get some more impression of the person's situation — then there is an increased rustling from the solicitors waiting for their cases to be heard, restlessness in the public gallery as family and friends want to know what's happening, and frowns from the court officials as they look meaningfully at their watches and the amount of paper work still waiting to be done. If the case has to be put back to another day so that more background information can be obtained, that is more time and expense. And, at the end of the day, it may still be the case that a fine is the eventual outcome anyway.

If a sentencer tries to do something unusual or more imaginative, then the result can be guaranteed to be in the next day's headlines. One Scottish sheriff has made something of a reputation on the basis of one or two cases in which distinctive use has been made of a deferred sentence. People have been ordered to write essays, take music lessons, bake cakes, buy their wives presents, and so on. A feature of these decisions has been some attempt to relate the task very directly to the circumstances of the offence and the offender.

These more exceptional examples serve to underline the more general experience of sentencers that their task is a mechanical, limited, constrained, and often frustrating and frustrated exercise.

Unpaid Fines

80% of disposals in Scottish courts involve fines. The majority of these are paid without the case having to come back to court. However, enforcing those which are not paid is a substantial problem. Very few alternatives to prison are available.

Up to a half of all admissions into Scottish prisons are for unpaid fines. Many of the amounts are small. Many of the offences were not serious ones. *It is the poorest, financially and socially, who are unable to "buy themselves out"* (ADSW Report, 1987).

Putting off the Evil Day

There is always a temptation to "defer sentence", and often many persuasive arguments put in court as to why to do this. The hesitation is that, in the absence of any real purpose for so doing, the sentencer is in fact ducking the basic problem — he or she is there to pass sentence. Often it is found that the hoped for job doesn't materialise, the steady girlfriend is steady no more — and the passage of time has simply reduced the options.

Probation and Community Service

There is a widespread complaint amongst sentencers in Scotland that probation is either not suggested often enough by social workers, or suggested in the wrong cases. There are also major resource problems in Scotland about the funding of probation work. A 1985 study found that spending on probation in Scotland was about a third of what it "should" have been in comparison with England and Wales (Joint Review Group on Services to Offenders, 1985, unpublished). From April 1991, probation work will be changed to become funded 100% by Central Government. It remains to be seen whether the funds earmarked will be sufficient to permit any great expansion of its use.

Community service is a very popular measure with sentencers. It meets a number of different aims in the one order. Its very popularity puts a real pressure on the number of work placements available. Community service was introduced in 1972, and it was emphasised that it should be an alternative to a prison sentence. However the law does not require a court to make a prison sentence and then substitute a community service order; rather it lets the court make such an order in any case in which prison was a possible penalty, and it is in a great many! So it is always tempting to stretch a point because of community service's attractions. But this is a short sighted policy. The chickens can come home to roost very quickly when the community service organiser comes along to announce that the scheme has no vacancies just when the ideal case presents itself.

Headlong into Prison — A Typical Scenario

Prison is supposed to be the place of last resort. The law requires sentencers in many cases to get a social work report, and to consider alternatives suggested in it, before they can legally impose a custodial sentence. Even so, the most well disposed sentencer often finds himself or herself sending someone to prison.

There comes before the court a young offender on a relatively minor charge of theft. On the face of it, prison does not, and should not, feature at all. But the story turns out differently ...

The young man admits he did it. His previous record is put before the court, and it transpires that he has three previous convictions for the same kind of thing in the last 18 months.

At this point the Clerk of Court tells the sentencer that the young man stills owes £100 of his fines from these previous occasions, and has not been paying them. Another fine for this offence starts to look impractical.

His solicitor tells the court that he has been unemployed for the last 12 months. Male unemployment in the town is about 15%, and his record of theft will not help him job hunting. Thus the prospect of exacting the money owed looks impractical. The sentencer could remit the earlier fines, if there were some special reason, but cannot substitute a different penalty for them. Fines have to be paid, or time served in lieu.

There is a report from a social worker. It tells of various domestic difficulties and family relationship problems. He was under supervision when younger, and responded quite well. However the report offers little idea of what probation might achieve. It also says that the priority such an order would be given would be low, in view of staffing difficulties in the office, and the relative non-seriousness of the offence.

The community service team have also submitted a report. He is seen as suitable for community service, and there is a vacancy. However the report reminds the court that community service places are scarce and that this offence is relatively minor. It warns that if community service orders are made in cases of this kind, placements will not be available for more serious ones.

And so, the young man goes to jail . . .

Conclusion

Sentencers dispose "justice", though there is much confusion as to what that means. The sentencer's own experience can be one of loneliness, constraint, and frustration. You are expected to be an independent expert in "sentencing" with the minimum of training and little opportunity to discuss the issues with a wider audience. You are unable to answer back. You must not appear doubtful or uncertain. You see little of the outcome of your activity, except perhaps when one of your "failures" reappears before you. You have been dragged away from a fascinating legal career at the Bar or in private practice to perform an unglamorous public duty to no-one's satisfaction.

"Nothing works," says the researcher. "Prison doesn't deter or reform," says the official handbook. "There is no clear policy for sentencing," says a book written by one of your colleagues. The idea of rehabilitation has collapsed. Doing good to criminals has little public support.

If you try something new or innovative, you will be all over the next morning's papers. The Lord Advocate or the Lord Chancellor will be calling for reports about your decision. If you don't send people to prison when the public think you should, there will be a heap of mail sent to your chambers, and the local rag will be full of correspondence from "disgusted" citizens.

It you want to put someone on probation, the social worker says "unsuited" or "low priority". If you want to use community service, the organiser says "house full". And if you hope prison will "do them some good" then the Governor says "don't you believe it".

Thus contradiction, constraint, and frustration is the frequent experience of the sentencer.

The Prison Governor

If imprisonment is a "practice without a policy", what sense is a Prison Governor to make of his or her task? Is "locking them up" the be all and end all of the job?

Official Answer

"The purpose of training and treatment of convicted prisoners shall be to encourage and assist them to lead a good and useful life" — thus saith the Prison Rules. Officially, therefore, the idea of "rehabilitation" still holds sway. Words such as "training" and "treatment" give expression to this idea. The idea gave the Prison Governor a sense of purpose, and a hope that something worthwhile could be achieved in what otherwise might be a depressing job. If only the numbers could be held down, and if only the conditions could be improved, then one could battle on with a bit of confidence.

Whether the idea of "doing good" to prisoners finds much support with the public at large, or even with the person in the pew, is more debatable. Any revelation that prisoners have it "soft" is likely to lead to outrage and indignation. They went to prison to be punished. The official line that people went to prison *as* punishment, and not *for* punishment, is not a distinction that troubles many.

Distinctions such as this are not likely to cut much ice with some prisoners either, as we shall see in another section of this book. Few find that the loss of liberty is the only punishment that prison involves.

So the Prison Governor starts with an official line that is not shared at any deep level by large sections of the society that is imprisoning the person; that is not true to the experience of those imprisoned; and that is now in any event frequently regarded as out of date or discredited.

Reviewing the Official Line

There has been a lot of discussion in recent years in official circles about the purpose of prison. In turn this affects how a Governor may now view his or her role.

In the late 1970s, two writers suggested that all prison could achieve was "humane containment" (King and Morgan, *The Future of the Prison System*, 1980). Prisons should give up any other pretence and simply seek to hold people for as long as the courts decided, and to have humane conditions.

In 1979 the May Committee suggested the idea of "positive custody" instead. A lot of what went on in the name of rehabilitation was valuable, even if the theories that underpinned it were somewhat doubtful. The May Committee's formula for positive custody included "assisting them to respond and to contribute to society"; self-respect; minimising the harm caused by being removed from society; and "preparing them for and assisting them on discharge". (*Report of the Inquiry into the United Kingdom Prison Service*, 1979, HMSO)

More recent statements (1988/89) set out *various* aims of imprisonment, including references to rehabilitation. They include aims and purposes over and above keeping people inside for the due period of time — for example, providing as full a life as possible within prison; enabling people to keep links with their families; and again the idea of contributing to society, and receiving help geared towards being returned to the community. (Scottish Prison Service, *Business Plan*, 1988/9)

The most recent summary of this debate is the Mission Statement produced by the Scottish Prison Service. "The

Mission ... is to keep in custody those committed by the courts, to maintain good order in each prison, to look after inmates with humanity, and to help them to lead law-abiding and useful lives in custody and after release" (ibid).

An important new word that is creeping into these discussions is that of "opportunity" (Scottish Prison Service, *Opportunity and Responsibility*, 1990). Once the basics of security and good order are attained, the prison's job is to provide opportunities. What use prisoners make of these is their choice. They cannot and should not be forced into "treatment" or anything else. But there should be resources and facilities designed to make the rhetoric of the Mission statement a possible reality.

Rhetoric and Reality

To compare with these statements of the official line, here is a set of statements from people with substantial experience of being involved in the running of prisons, which reflect some of their conclusions (various sources, incorporating members of the group writing this book, contributions to papers and conferences organised and published by the Centre for Theology and Public Issues, and *Hansard*):

— "The penal system is the community's refuse bin for its misfits";
— "Prison merely provides a respite, for varying periods of time, from the activities of law-breakers";
— "Public opinion is not sympathetic to massive public expenditure on people who are deemed to be in the system as a result of their freely chosen patterns of social behaviour";
— "Imprisonment for alcoholics is simply an illustration of an embarrassed community playing for time";
— "A more unlikely environment for spiritual renewal than a prison is difficult to imagine";
— "Imprisonment by its very nature deprives the individual inmate of all the freedoms that make a meaningful life";
— "Prison is always a negative experience: never send anyone there because you think it will 'do them some good'";

— "Prison will never be anything but a graveyard of good intentions — not just the enemy of the prisoner, *it is the enemy of society*";
— "It would be quite wrong to claim that the prison system has failed quite simply because there is no consensus as to what it is supposed to be doing".

Women's Imprisonment

The "gender" factor is nowadays an automatic subject for discussion in most discourses, but it is perhaps understandable that in the context of the penal system the presumption is that we are talking about men. Relatively few women offend, and the even smaller number that go to prison find themselves in Scotland's best kept establishment.

Certain problems in the penal system described throughout this book are intensified when the focus is on women. The very fact that the system is male dominated and male defined in so many of its respects bears heavily on women's experience of it, and how their offending is viewed by personnel within the criminal justice system. Only very slowly are women being appointed to governor grade posts in men's prisons and vice versa.

Women who appear before courts are almost all petty offenders, the group for whom the system does least and has minimum resources and alternatives. There are relatively few "real" female criminals. The system is often dealing with serious mental health problems for which it has inadequate expertise. Many have alcohol and drug abuse problems, including those of legitimately prescribed tranquillisers and anti-depressants.

It can be assumed that almost all women have retained greater family responsibilities than men, with the consequent effect upon dependants in the event of incarceration. The placing of all women prisoners in the one establishment, however well kept, may not help the retention of links with family and children.

One possible compensation in this whole situation is that, with relatively low numbers, the prison service has been able to deal with women in small units. The evaluation of such an approach may hold the key to the way forward for other parts of the penal system.

The Contradictions of the Job

What prisons do well, on the whole, is to keep people in for the periods of time that the courts dictate. A Prison Governor knows that any escape will be the one thing guaranteed to put prison issues in the newspapers. The reverse side of this coin is that it induces resistance to practical schemes for "assisting prisoners to lead a good and useful life on discharge". "Many good schemes for rehabilitation have been scrapped due to an antipathy to take risks," said one Governor. Fear of public reaction, or of the known attitudes of a particular local community, can often restrict the taking of even the smallest risks.

The "political football" phenomenon in penal affairs is another restriction on Governors. The autonomy of Governors has been curtailed, or even eroded, by ever more layers of control at Central Government level. Politicians, who decide on policy, are averse to taking risks in the business of running prisons — especially if either their minister or the prison is in a marginal constituency. Yet staff from Governor downwards are daily taking decisions in high risk situations, and are expected to cope without embarrassing their masters. Any and every daily decision in prison life has unforeseen, possibly explosive, potential.

Trying to achieve rehabilitation in a prison setting is *possibly the biggest contradiction of all*. "It is the most difficult part of our task," wrote the previous Director of the Scottish Prison Service (Thomson, *Has the Prison System Failed?*, 1986, p. 62) "What we ask of our staff in this respect encapsulates the quandary in which the prison system as a whole finds itself," he wrote. The prison officer has to try to do two things which are well nigh incompatible. As custodian, the officer has to distance himself from his or her charges and exercise control over them. If, however, he or she is to aid rehabilitation, then relationships with prisoners have to be built, and relationships based on foundations *other than the exercise of authority*. This conundrum was expressed most famously in Paterson's dictum — "how do you train people for freedom in conditions of captivity?"

It's not just newspapers, politicians, and the job itself that make life difficult. At times the behaviour of prisoners stretches "do-gooding" and simple human tolerance beyond limits. There are limits to the human capacity for compassion in the face of the objectionable and insulting behaviour that is sometimes met from prisoners.

As Governor, you are on the receiving end of every grievance, whether real or imagined, that a person may have derived from a whole lifetime of treatment at the hands of authority figures. You have no control over the personal histories that prisoners bring into prison with them. Those histories, and the behaviour that results, are not of your making. Even the prisoner may have little control over them either.

It is the *range* of people and circumstances which needs emphasis. Prisons are not full of the "animals", "monsters" or "devils" so beloved of the popular press. At any one time there will be some very dangerous people in prison. However, cheek by jowl with them will be the socially immature, the inadequate, and the mentally unstable. Equally there is no shortage of apparently self-confident, assertive individuals who are born survivors. To outward appearances, nothing, just nothing, touches them. Many just want a quiet life, and to get out as quickly as possible. Others are conducting some kind of private war against society and all it stands for. One cliché, born of the popular press, is perhaps more accurate — "all human life is there".

Perhaps the final contradiction is an expectation that prison will indeed cure the problems that brought the person into prison and which lie outside the prison altogether. Many prisoners return to society sincerely believing that they will not offend again. Yet their good intentions are soon overwhelmed by that same set of personal and social problems which contributed to their offence in the first place. The cumulative effect of environment, background, family pressures, group loyalties, unemployment, alcoholism, addiction, and a host of other factors will all frequently bring to nought the best efforts of both staff and prisoner.

If the prison or the Governor is accused of failure, it is only fair to ask what problems they were being expected to resolve in the first place.

Conclusion

There are conflicting expectations of what prison can or should achieve. Objectives that have official blessing may not have much public support. Fear of public reaction militates against risk taking.

The search is on for a formula to replace the traditional ideology of rehabilitation. There is little involvement from the outside community, and from the churches. Confronted with "all sorts and conditions of people", Governors are asked to solve the unsolvable, and are then criticised when they fail.

At a recent conference, the Bishop of Lincoln underlined the responsibility of society for the situation in our prisons (*The Meaning of Imprisonment*, 1989, p. 46). "We need," he said, "to recognise that the abuse of justice in our prisons continues to repose for the most part on the lazy, unreflecting belief of the general public that prisoners deserve nothing better. I consider that most of the issues in penal affairs are fundamentally theological. They are about justice and forgiveness, reconciliation and hope. For no one in his right mind wants to be a mere administrator of the penal machine, or a lion tamer in one of society's cages."

The Prison Officer

"I joined the prison service 22 years ago to enhance my status and perform what I considered to be a very responsible job. I saw myself as having the personal qualities necessary to influence and advise individuals who were unlikely to have had the benefit of a stable home background like my own. Given the opportunity, I felt sure that I could mirror my inherent principles and relate them to the situation in which my new charges had now found themselves," wrote a prison officer (submission prepared for the group writing this book).

What was his experience of the system? "I did not, however, take account of the forces at work within an unnatural enviroment." His conclusion was that, over time, young officers, optimistic and eager to change the system in a positive way, *become passionate defenders of the status quo.*

These are some of the forces he listed of which he did not take account, and which produce this effect:

1 In order to survive and gain acceptance from their peers, prisoners operate a range of rules and procedures *from which prison officers are excluded.* There is a subculture among prisoners. Part of it involves the very understandable desire to gain access to the widest range of privileges, and prisoners will, in general, use whatever means are available to attain these ends. In some contexts outside prison this kind of behaviour might be praised as "use of initiative" or "being enterprising". In prison it is perceived by staff as "manipulation" which has to be countered.

2 There is also a staff subculture, and other colleagues have to be satisfied that their positions are not being compromised. All this leads to rigid interpretations of prison rules; this ensures consistency of approach, but reduces flexibility. It ends up by frustrating the prisoner even more. It all comes as a rude shock to the officer's best intentions and good motives in wanting to join up in the first place.

3 The general trend of deference to authority once prevalent in the prison system has disappeared. The raising of material aspirations over the last 10 years, coupled in some cases with decreasing opportunities and means to attain them, have their impact on prisoners. The education system encourages young people to be questioning and not simply to accept what they are told. The system, however, still expects deference from inmates.

4 *The most difficult area is in the field of "relationships".* It is all very well for the officer to seek a meaningful relationship with a prisoner. But what about the prisoner?

The framework for the relationship is derived from the prison as an organisation, and he cannot negotiate the parameters of it as a result. He maybe cannot afford to embark on relationships, even if he wanted to. To make a relationship meaningful, both parties should ideally be free to negotiate its content. This option is simply not available because of the bureaucratic structure of the organisation, and the forces at work in the subcultures both of the prisoner and of the prison officer.

One institution visited by members of the group writing this book had suffered mass disturbances. Its status had been changed, as part of a policy called "Grand Design", in order to help relieve overcrowding in other parts of the system. It had built up a relatively liberal régime, in its own eyes. According to the staff, other prisons sent some of their most troublesome prisoners, who abused this régime. The result was a series of confrontations and serious disturbances which led to a severe lock-down policy, which took its toll upon staff and inmates alike.

The lesson that staff frequently draw from such incidents is that *control is paramount*. All else must be secondary. Whilst a "liberal" régime is preferable to a "repressive" one, it is seen as inherently open to abuse and loss of control. However, a number of staff were nostalgic for what they saw as the more positive régimes of the former borstals and detention centres. They felt that these allowed certain skills and values to be instilled, and for more positive relations between staff and inmates to develop. *The sense of doing something positive, from which people could benefit, was missing from current régimes.*

Staff who join the service come to find that there are massive obstacles to doing the good and valuable things they might have wanted to do by joining up. They are forced, by the nature of the system, into roles and situations which make for confrontation, and a climate of opposition between staff and inmates. The natural preoccupation, both personal and institutional, with control and security severely limits the scope for personal relationships and the terms on which anything other than a stereotyped relationship can be built up.

One officer said it all: "I thought I would change the system, but the system has changed me".

The Prison Chaplain

"I'm not religious, but . . ." is often the opening someone uses as an overture to the chaplain. It can be the "way in" for the person to start talking about the things which matter most deeply. These may not be "religious" matters in the common sense of the word. But the discussion may lead to a relationship in which remorse can be expressed, and through which there may come liberation from false attitudes and expectations, and an experience of acceptance, forgiveness, and healing. Can the chaplain break through where others, because of their official role, are more hamstrung?

The Chaplain's Inheritance

In Victorian times the chaplain had a place second only to the Governor and the Medical Officer. The chaplain was expected to use the establishment's authority to persuade the inmates to practise the Christian religion, breaches of which had brought them into prison in the first place. Prisons, after all, were "penitentiaries". In turn it was believed that religion would reinforce respect for the law, and would help health and hygiene.

Today no such religious consensus exists. Few people reveal their beliefs in public and fewer would want them imposed on prisoners. One chaplain wrote, "religion is not highly attractive outside and therefore we can hardly expect it to be very attractive inside. God isn't a high profile person in our society and therefore he is unlikely to be high profile in the prison. We should be glad that we are so 'tolerated' in prison by both staff and prisoners" (Submission to the group writing this book).

Nevertheless, chaplains still enjoy a special status. They are unique in being appointed by a body completely independent of the prison. That they can immediately pick up a key is an anomaly, and to some an anachronism. Indeed prison statutes expect chaplains to see all admissions, those confined to bed, and those on punishment. Reports from chaplains' meetings indicate that much of this is not done, and indeed cannot be done.

There is a debate about the chaplain's role. Until recently it was understood that chaplains were there to serve prisoners. Now, however, there is the idea that the chaplain should be appointed to the prison as such. This suggests that the chaplain might be seen as a member of a team, including other prison staff such as social workers and educationalists. It also suggests that chaplains might see themselves as having a role in relation to the whole institution.

The Chaplain's Experience of Prison

Initial impressions are of the apparent pettiness of prison, and the noise within the insitution. But then comes admiration and gratitude for the way that chaplains' work is accommodated. Chaplains find that they can wander through the prison and talk to everyone. They find that most people will talk to them.

Then comes awareness of the craziness of the system; of the numbers around who should not be there; of the many who are sick or immature or handicapped; of so many who are drunkards or drug cases. Questions follow about other issues — parole, consistency in sentencing, of how long a life sentence should be, of preparation for the outside — of what else needs to be done.

A woman chaplain in a male prison felt that anxiety was the greatest effect that prisons have on the people in them. Officers felt the anxiety associated with the need of the community to treat the prisoner as a scapegoat, *and the undesirable side-effects this can have.* The lack of purpose in what should be done with people serving prison sentences may so often lead to the explosive tension of boredom and fear.

Her experience was also that prisoners have a high level of general anxiety which goes with sentencing and admission to prison. Sentences may be felt to be unjust, and there is concern that those thought to be friends would desert. There is the awareness of the pressures on the family, and of local community reaction — of children growing up with only one parent. There is fear that the Police may make life difficult on release. There is anxiety about future re-offending because of a society which will be rejecting of them on release.

For many prisoners, the helping agencies are compromised by their statutory role. On the other hand the chaplain is seen as a friend who will keep confidences — "I would presume that any prisoner could talk with me about anything and that was it; it shouldn't affect their parole or their reports". However, if the chaplain is to have a role in relation to staff as well as to prisoners, can this still be the case?

It is said that the chaplain is the one who offers an unconditional relationship to all prisoners, because chaplains have no need to distinguish between innocent and guilty. Chaplains need to convey this sense of independence if they are to remain credible. But they run the risk of seeming to be against the establishment. One chaplain wanted to avoid being on the side of anyone, whether prisoner or staff. He saw himself as not being part of the system and hoping he could remain apart as an outsider, still able to minister to all parties.

Possible Roles of the Chaplain

"Loitering with intent" was quoted as one description of chaplains' work. Being seen around so that it is as easy as possible to be approached. In providing this presence, chaplains see themselves as representatives of the church. In all the comments, the conduct of worship in prison was mentioned but seldom, and the recruitment of new members for their respective denominations not at all — functions which the outsider, and possibly the average church member, might have initially expected to be the chaplain's *raison d'être*.

The woman chaplain in a male prison found that she could play an important part in helping to lower the levels of anxiety. Often a woman is seen as a "safe" figure — and women are increasingly being appointed to governor grade posts in men's prisons in Scotland — and the prisoner may feel able to drop the "hard man" image. Male prisons do not on the whole offer much outlet for the expression of tender feelings.

"Your chapel choir seems to be mostly beasts" was one comment expressed to this same chaplain. Again her experience was that sex offenders and those caught up in homosexuality in prison tended to feel less threatened by a woman, and so *there was the possibility of conversation, the building up of self esteem, the looking together at the change of life style.*

Another chaplain described the role in the following terms: "He is around; he is different. All ministry calls us to be in some way a person of God. A light in darkness; someone who releases a drop of hope; who accepts people and every person as a whisper from God. Who believes in the dignity of all, and therefore no one is beyond hope; no one is scum, no one can be written off. We seem to be dangerous amateurs prowling. . . ."

The Chaplain and Churches

Few chaplains find a sympathetic chord when they speak, even to their own congregations, about the needs of prisoners. Even in discussions among Christians about prisons, the role of chaplains is seldom mentioned. Essentially it appears to be understood as a sacred function, responsible primarily for Sunday worship and individual follow-up, rather independent of the general régime. Comments on rehabilitation, for example, appear to assume that this will be done in a mainly secular context, e.g. through counselling.

One chaplain accounted for this experience as follows: "Part of the reason for the detachment of churches from prison work is that the churches increasingly cater for people who see themselves as part of the more respectable part of society. They are unlikely to have had first hand contact with the majority of people who end up in prison. Nor have the churches much of a profile in human rights, and demands for prison reforms have not met with much sympathy from the churches."

Out of Isolation?

The chaplain can feel very isolated. He or she is appointed in a unique way to work in the prison, and has an uncertain role. The role is clearly not the establishment one of the Victorian era, but it is not quite certain what it is. Whether it is for the prisoner (and his or her family), or for the prison, various dilemmas ensue. Perhaps the hardest part of all is that the chaplain *may feel most isolated from the very community, the church, that he or she represents.*

One solution may be an ecumenical one. "We have chosen to work as an ecumenical team, sharing the one chapel for all Christian worship. This goes a long way to communicate the team concept to both staff and inmates, many of whom are locked within the Protestant/Roman Catholic chaplain pattern. I believe that the team approach has also made it easier for a woman to be accepted into prison chaplaincy. Indeed it may well be that a team of male and female chaplains within an institution, such as a prison, may show the way forward in our thinking towards future patterns of ministry" (Submission by member of the group writing this book).

The Psychiatrist

If the job of the criminal justice system is to punish people who have committed crimes, then it has to determine that they are *guilty* before it can do so. The sentencer, the prison governor, and the social worker, only have a role to play in the system if it has been decided that someone is guilty of a crime or an offence. On this way of looking at things, society is the innocent party — it has been offended against. The sentence, or punishment, is how it deals with someone whom it finds to be guilty. The focus is on deeds, and society deals with the guilty by punishing them for those deeds.

The psychiatrist comes into this system with a very different way of looking at things. The psychiatrist is aware of the *sharp contrasts* between this approach in the criminal justice system, and that of his or her own profession. Yet it is not so simple as that. At various points in its workings, the criminal justice system finds roles for the psychiatrist to perform. It finds ways of accommodating the insights of psychiatry and using them. The complexities can serve to raise the issue of *how to deal with guilt.*

The Law's Approach to Guilt

The law begins by assuming that people normally act freely and intentionally. It holds them responsible for their actions. The question of their *"mens rea"* — i.e. whether they "meant" their actions — is decided by the court on the basis of a legal approach. What the person says about what they intended or meant may not have a lot to do with what the law decides as to their guilt.

However, there are some circumstances in which there may be a question as to the person's level of responsibility and intentionality. In these circumstances psychiatrists may be involved in the legal process in the determination of this question. The law includes a concept of "insanity", and uses psychiatric opinion in defining it; two people who commit the same act, but have different degrees of responsibility/ sanity may end up in quite different places — one in prison, and the other in mental hospital. There is also the issue of "diminished responsibility", which can also bear on the outcome of the case. Various factors — for example, chemical imbalance, brain disorder, emotional disturbance — may be involved in affecting the degree of "voluntariness" with which the law normally assumes they behave.

The law decides whether someone is guilty by the formal process of a trial. The conduct of any trial is determined by rules and regulations laid down in the law, or by previous decisions in like cases. In any proof, the central concern is with evidence, from external facts and sources, that the person committed the crime. The thoughts, felt intentions, or particular psychology of the person on trial may be secondary to the determination of their guilt.

However, the law's approach cannot simply be determined by reference to statutes, or books of rules and regulations. How serious some behaviour is regarded as being cannot be assessed simply by seeing what penalties the law sets for it.

Views fluctuate over time as to the function of law in a society: should it enforce a code that expresses a certain view of life and morals held by a dominant section of society; or should it be essentially regulatory, allowing people the maximum liberty, providing they do not abuse it or harm others?

In daily practice a lot depends on the myriad practitioners, prosecutors, lawyers, and judges operating the system. Some behaviours may occasion a greater sense of "offence" in some communities or areas than in others. Some kinds of offences may be particularly prevalent at one particular point in time. At a practical level the law ordinarily takes into account any "mitigating" factors around a particular offence or offender. A court will look to any expression of remorse that it feels is genuine as mitigation. It may also acknowledge, for example, if it has had to obtain a social worker's report on the person's background and family circumstances, that allocating responsibility is not so straightforward as it may at first appear.

However, on the whole the law is concerned with attributing guilt to people on the basis of what they have done, and with dealing with that guilt by imposing a punishment on them. What the person themselves may feel in terms of guilt, or think about the crime, may not be a central factor in the business. The law's use of the word "process" has to do with "due process" — the application of rules and regulations set out in books or determined by tribunals of various kinds.

The Approach from Psychiatry

It is a person's *inner* world of thoughts and feelings that is the central interest of the psychiatrist. In any understanding of behaviour the psychiatrist will be very conscious of a person's mental processes, the ways in which they think and feel, and especially the significance of early relationships in their life. In the psychiatrist's experience, a person's sense of guilt, or what they feel in the way of responsibility, will only partly be affected by any legal proceedings they may have undergone.

If the person is to deal with their feelings of guilt, then, from the psychiatrist's perspective, *they need to be in a relationship* with someone in which they can give expression to their feelings. They may need help with even starting to express those feelings, let alone getting around to exploring other possible ways of behaving that do not involve breaking the law. The "process" in which the psychiatrist is interested is in how the *person* works through their feelings and deals with them. Once society has "done its thing" and pronounced them guilty, the person concerned has to come to terms with that, and with whatever guilt they feel about the offence.

The process can last much longer than any court hearing, or even a prison sentence. There has to be a sense of safety in talking to someone, a need to be able to trust them. There has to be confidentiality. Different stages of the process may need to occur with different people, or at different times as people are ready to explore more of their reactions and feelings about their crime.

Different parts of the story may not come out until much later. The process may not be one continuous event — there may be fallow periods, then sudden breakthroughs. Even in ideal circumstances, dealing with guilt, from the psychiatrist's perspective, is a complex matter. It needs to occur in the context of a safe relationship.

Dealing with Guilt

The workings of the system often serve to exacerbate the difficulties in the process of acknowledging, accepting, and dealing with guilt.

People may have a whole series of "defence mechanisms" which they use in order to avoid admitting their guilt, or to justify their wrong-doing, or to immunise themselves against experiencing the feelings that others may expect them to have.

Court procedure is formal and rigid. Courts are suspicious of the expressions of feelings. Lawyers may find the idea that responsibility is affected by early relationships and social factors does not sit easily with legal approaches to guilt.

In prison, time and energy are taken up with sheer survival. There is often a lot of movement between prisons during sentence, which interrupts relationships that may be just building up. Dealing with the here and now situation becomes the preoccupation, not contemplating one's feelings of guilt, or thinking about future behaviour.

In prison there is a hierarchy regarding crimes. Lowest in the pecking order are sex offenders against children, then perhaps "granny bashers". Fellow prisoners can be more punitive than people outside. Those who it might be thought needed to explore very deep and painful feelings about their offence get most hassle, and least opportunity. What the person learns is precisely how to deny and fabricate in order to survive.

Staff may have unresolved feelings or prejudices of their own about certain offences — they are as human as anyone else. It takes a prisoner a long time to know who to trust, and to whom it is safe to talk about sensitive subjects. And there is the uncertainty about how, if the truth is told, and feelings admitted, it will affect the chance of early release.

What people feel in the way of guilt, or about offending, is influenced by factors far beyond the walls of the prison, and the operations of the criminal justice system. Those working in the system, on society's behalf, come across people who are as offended against as have offended, *or who may feel no sense of belonging to that society at all.*

There are many people who do not feel guilt at all. The absence of guilt may be not so much pathological as normal. Because of the area they come from, or because of their particular life experiences, or a combination of both, they feel no investment in the wider society at all. They know what they did is against that society's law, but they have little if any feeling that what they did was wrong, in their own eyes.

There is a whole series of distinctions between public and private morality which affect people's sense of guilt. Stealing from institutions is less serious than stealing from a person; they could afford it; everybody does it — I just got caught.

Immaturity among prisoners is often met, or it may be that an immature part of the person's psyche bears on their offending. Discrepancy between chronological age and emotional maturity is part of the human condition. But maturation is enabled crucially through developing relationships.

Some people can derive a very distorted or excessive sense of guilt as a result of early life experiences, or the dynamics of the relationships in their family life. Guilt feelings carry over into later life, so that some people carry excessive guilt feelings that are in no way justified by their offence.

Peer group pressure, or personal loyalties, can require people to "take the rap" for the crime of a partner or associate. No sense of guilt is met here. A set of values is operating here that is outside the bounds either of psychiatry, or of the criminal justice system.

The Psychiatrist's Experience

The psychiatrist working in prison is faced with a wide range of people, and of diagnostic categories. There may be patients psychotic, brain-damaged, alcohol addicted, personality disordered, and those grossly distressed by prison and the events surrounding it. The job is to make an assessment and implement action. There may be some who need treatment in a mental hospital, and there is legislation to enable that to occur. The main constraints are the existing provision for treating prisoners in those hospitals.

Wandering around the local jail, one is impressed, not by the neglected lunatics but by the flotsam and jetsam of society, who, day in and day out, wander in and out, and in and out. Thirty days, three months, seven days was one prisoner's sequence on his record. He may drink and misbehave, he may steal; she may shoplift; he may expose himself in public; she may breach the peace when high on drugs, or just plain upset.

It is obvious that these people are not suitable for jail. They were in the wrong place in the large Victorian mental hospitals, and now they are in the wrong place in jail. Why were reception centres not developed? Why so few designated places for the intoxicated? Where are the probation and after-care hostels and extended care systems that are required?

These people are often called "psychiatric", and to an extent they are. They do not, however, merit the treatment that the acute psychotic does, for example, and as such are unwelcome as in-patients. Among them are people who once had a reasonable personality, but due to illness or trauma, it was damaged and is now severely limited. They drift into poverty. *They are a nuisance, maybe, but not a danger to society.* We keep them behind high walls and burden prison staff with them. Their dignity and that of their carers is impugned by this process. The prisons' ability to manage the more dangerous is prejudiced by the on-going demands of this group. The psychiatrist can contribute by removing the most disturbed of them, but *the limitations of most psychiatrists visiting prison are considerable.*

Dealing with "Badness"

Society deals with people it decides are "bad" by punishing them for their misdeeds. It puts them away, either literally or metaphorically. Through its legal processes it may take minimal account of their intentions, thoughts, feelings, and background. Having imposed the punishment, it may have little further interest in what the person feels about having been so branded, in what the punishment does to them, and about how they deal with all of that.

Dealing with those feelings of badness can involve for the person concerned depression, despair, suicidal feelings, and self-loathing. When "defences" of a psychological kind are broken down, some pretty raw areas of the personality can be exposed. Yet the defences may need to be broken down if new patterns of behaviour are to emerge. New relationships can be faced, and difficult feelings confronted, in the context of a trusting relationship.

"Locking away" is a mechanism that the community uses as well in relation to feelings about offences and offenders. Society may project its sense of disgust on to the person in the dock. Just as a prisoner may work hard to avoid admitting the crime, so may the community resist acknowledging its own feelings of badness about offenders. These defences on the part of the community may need to be broken down, as much as those of any prisoner. Maybe out of that breaking down, a new relationship between society and its offenders could emerge.

The Social Worker/Probation Officer

"Dare to Care" is the motto of the Scottish Prison Service. The social work and probation services might do well to adopt it as their motto too. An act of caring is becoming an act of daring, even in the so-called "caring" services. For the probation officer/social worker there is a very acute sense of crisis and tension at the present time. The basic values and philosophy on which these services are based are questioned.

Scotland's approach to dealing with juvenile delinquency (the Children's Hearing System) is unique in Western Europe and attracts international attention. It is a "welfare" and not a "punishment" system. Scotland's system of including probation services for older offenders along with other social services in one all-purpose department of the local authority is also unique in Western Europe. But it does not seem to have heralded any radical, large scale, trans-formation of the way adult delinquency is dealt with. As from April 1991, the system of funding local authority services for offenders will change, but what the approach adopted by social workers will be remains to be seen.

For England and Wales, the government has given some very clear indications of its thinking. For some groups of people in need in our society, the job of social workers and their agencies has been set out in a document called *Care in the Community* (HMSO, 1990). But the way that the government wants probation officers and social workers in the criminal justice system to work is set out in a document entitled 'Punishment in the community' (Home Office, 1988). *Social workers are to be carers in one context, but punishers in another.*

At first sight the intention of reducing the number of people sent to prison, which is the avowed intention, seems laudable. Putting the probation and social work services in the front line of that approach should be attractive to those services. *But the approach is still based on making the idea of punishment central.* Moreover the flavour of that idea is given away by the associated buzz words such as "toughening up" the various orders; talking of "hard physcical tasks" that offenders must perform; inserting tight "conditions" that they must meet very stringently; by talk of "curfews" and "tagging".

Moreover the kind of values basic to social work are being overtaken by the values of the market place and the language of competition and privatisation. Probation and social work have been invaded by the three "E"s — efficiency, effectiveness, and economy. Values of humanity, compassion, persistence that cannot be put into a financial equation are played down in this framework. The only time the word "value" is now heard is in the phrase "value for money".

Where Social Work came in

The first social workers in the criminal justice system were quite avowedly people with a *mission* (King, *The Probation Service*, 1969; Haxby, *Probation a Changing Service*, 1976).

Whether the evil was drink, or prison, or the sentences of the court, these were people on a rescue mission. They wanted to keep people out of prison. They were very clear about their values and ways of working with people. Their inspiration and motivation were drawn from religious and moral fervour. They wanted the courts to entrust people to their care, and to their strongly held beliefs in the effectivess of a caring and humanistic approach. *Their* "mission statements" were not written in government documents.

Out of this initiative came the idea of probation as we now know it. The idea combines the elements of control and care in a simple but effective formula. It has stood the test of time, having first been put on the statute books in 1907/8 (Moore and Wood, *Social Work and Criminal Law in Scotland*, 1981, pp. 100 *et seq*). It is a flexible and versatile measure:

> Society, through the court order and the supervision exercised by the officer/worker keeps its eye on the

person. A sanction is held over them in case they get into further trouble or don't keep the terms of the order. Extra conditions can be put into the order, directed both towards others (such as restitution, or, in Scotland, unpaid work), or to the needs and problems of the person themselves (such as to get treatment for alcoholism).

People get an opportunity to live down their offences. They may be getting an opportunity to avoid going to prison. They are put in the way of resources and help which they may need to help them cope with life in general, and especially to keep out of trouble.

The social worker/probation officer has a clear framework in which to offer care and social work services consistent with his or her motivation and professionalism. The social worker is clearly recognised as being involved not to administer punishment for its own sake, but to operate the care which is his or her *raison d'être*. The definition of the first Probation Act has never been bettered. The job was to "supervise, advise, assist, and befriend" the person. Not to be a "screw on wheels".

Probation work developed from its beginnings with missionary individuals and charitable societies into a separately organised service. It became a formal part of the system. Funding, and associated inspection and control, came from central and local government. The courts had an important share in responsibility for the service at local level. The service also became more professional. The officers received training in psychology and the social sciences. They became the court's "experts" in the treatment of offenders.

The courts began to make increasing use of the services of probation officers and social workers. As confidence in them increased, older and more serious offenders were tried out on probation. Laws came in to make courts use social work reports when they were sentencing people, whether or not probation was in their minds.

The work developed in other directions too. Responsibility for people released from prisons on various licences passed to probation officers and social workers. Some staff moved to work in penal establishments alongside prison officers and governors.

Different ways of working with people developed. Groups of offenders might be seen together, as well as for individual discussions.

Volunteers from the community were drawn in to help in various ways — assisting prisoners' families; providing a particular type of "befriending" to some offenders; and in a whole host of imaginative ways.

In the 1970s a new idea was floated — community service — which was then introduced into the legislation as a separate sentence. Probation officers and social workers were given the job of working out how to implement this new idea. They brought to the task a humanistic approach: in some instances they developed imaginative ways of bringing offenders into touch with other people in the community. Offenders became "helpers" as well as "helped".

All this illustrates that plenty of scope was found by people in the system to make use of social work and social work approaches. The various legal orders — probation, community service, after-care licence — seemed to give an adequate sanction for the authorities, and ample scope for social workers to operate realistic, practical, caring and humane approaches to people in trouble.

Probation Work in Scotland

There is no separate probation service in Scotland, as it is known in England and Wales. Since 1969, all the tasks we have been discussing have been undertaken by social workers employed by Local Authority Social Work Departments. These departments are also responsible for providing social work services to every group in need in the community, and for every kind of social and personal problem — "from the cradle to the grave," it is often said.

At least three points in favour of this system can be claimed. First, the social work identity of the service for people in trouble is enhanced and emphasised by this arrangement. Second, people in trouble are less stigmatised in that they go to the same office as anyone else in need, and not to some separate "probation" office. And third, that the local community, through its democratically elected local authority, is responsible for people in trouble, and not a rather separate criminal justice system; in turn people in trouble are eligible as of right, and have access through their social worker to resources and services available to the whole community.

However, in spite of these advantages, *two fundamental problems remain with this arrangement.*

First, services for people in trouble have to compete for resources with those for other groups of people whose needs are seen as more urgent or more deserving. From a councillor's point of view, there are few votes to be won in this kind of work. The idea of the community being responsible for its offenders may be largely rhetoric. Services for children and the elderly would certainly command greater priority in the eyes of the general public. And the motivation of many people entering social work is such that working with offenders is not likely to be their main interest. When resources for local authorities generally have become tighter, services for offenders struggle even to maintain their own.

Second, the system of funding for local authority services does not generally allow for the "earmarking" of money for particular parts of the services, or special groups of "clients". The theory is that local authorities should be relatively free to set their own priorities. However, community service orders for offenders only got started in Scotland when central government set aside some money to allow them happen. Development of even what offender services do exist has been uneven and unbalanced.

The new arrangements that are to be introduced as from April 1991, will involve 100% funding by central government of all social work services for offenders, so at least the imbalance can be corrected and an appropriate policy be developed.

Thus there is a fine rhetoric about probation services in Scotland, but one that is not always matched by reality. In the mid 1980s, a study showed that only a third was being spend on offender services of what "should" have been spent on a comparative basis with England and Wales (Joint Review Group on Services to Offenders, 1985, unpublished). The worries are that, if the only way of getting probation services provided in Scotland is by 100% government funding:

1) will the money be enough to make up for the years of neglect and under-funding?
2) will the government insist in Scotland, as in England and Wales, on "national standards" that give expression to its emphasis on "punishment"?
3) will sentencers and social workers develop a new understanding of what probation services will involve to help bring about a reduction in the numbers sent to prison?

The Collapse of a Model in Probation Work

Like the sentencer and the prison governor, the social worker/probation officer has been affected by the collapse of the rehabilitative model. The "expert" status of the social worker in this field was tied very closely to a particular set of theories, and to ways of working with people based on them.

The approach drew heavily on ideas derived from psychiatry. It focussed very closely on the relationship between the officer and the person under supervision as the vehicle through which the objectives of the order were to be achieved. The danger was that the means — the "relationship" — could become sacrosanct, and the ends were lost sight of. Probation officers and social workers have had to respond to the criticisms being made of this exclusivity of method. Three aspects of the problem can be given to illustrate the kinds of issues involved:

1 The language of "treatment" suggests that crime is something "wrong" with the person, that has to be "cured". This approach could neglect all the family and social pressures that might have influenced the offence. It also appeared to excuse the offender of responsibility, if he was in some way "ill".
2 As attention shifted more to social and group influences on people's offending, social workers had to persuade courts that different methods of work should be used in

c

probation work. Building up a relationship through regular meetings with the person fitted very well with the court's interest in "keeping an eye" on someone. But group work, or family centred work, was less familiar.

3 In the prison context, ideas such as "humane containment", or "positive custody", or the "opportunity" model, were discussed as alternatives to replace the idea of "rehabilitation".

In probation work the discussions tended to suggest that the "punishment" aspects (for example, turning out regularly to report to the probation officer), should be separated from the social work "help" that was to be attempted. The social work was to be negotiated on a more voluntary basis with the person, so that it wasn't forced on them. Does this separation represent a travesty of the basic idea of probation?

Social workers and probation officers did diversify their practice. From different kinds of theories they developed different kinds of approaches and focusses. This in turn enhanced their ability to take on a wider range of people and problems, still within the basic framework of court orders, such as probation and community service. *The important point is that social work values and approaches remained central.* If people don't take the opportunity offered, or the advantage of them, the courts always have the sanction to call them back and impose another decision. But the prime purpose of the orders social workers and probation officers administer is not the imposition of punishment as an end in its own right. The orders are a penalty imposed by the courts, and some aspects of them (reporting, working, helping others, paying back money) involve deprivation for the offender. But the prime purpose is humane and helpful, both for the offender and for society.

The Experience of the Social Worker/Probation Officer

The social worker, like the psychiatrist, comes into the criminal justice system with a set of values and approaches that are intrinsic to the caring professions. The social worker will be as conscious of the significance of early relationships, personal feelings, and private meanings of the individual in trouble as the psychiatrist. The social worker will be aware of the impact that the person's family and social circumstances make upon the person's life and attitudes. The social worker/probation officer is also likely to be motivated by a passion about the negative effects of imprisonment, and concern about the extent to which it is used. He or she will be committed to concepts of probation and community service as alternative and more humane ways of dealing with people in trouble.

What he or she finds is a legal system set up to punish, a public view of anything other than prison as a soft option or a let off, and a mood which wants to turn social workers and probation officers into "screws on wheels" — and moreover a "screw" that carries its calculator about with it to see if it is "worth" trying to help the person. The values of "advising, assisting, and befriending" seem to have little place in today's discourse.

In Scotland the social worker finds additionally that work with people in trouble is "low priority", that many colleagues came into social work without any awareness that this was part of social work, and that he or she is accountable to a group of councillors who may not regard offenders as part of their "constituency".

There is just a chance in Scotland that the new funding arrangements could provide an opportunity to break out of the limitations that have applied in recent years. But taking advantage of that opportunity will require that social workers and their departments have an idea of what it is that they want to do, that will drive their structures and activity.

There is still the vacuum of ideas that has to be filled, as well as filling the coffers to make it possible to realise those ideas.

The Agenda for Probation a Hundred Years on

A hundred years ago probation began with people with fire in their bellies being concerned about prison conditions and prison use, and about the evils of drink and poverty as factors in the causation of crime. They took initiatives in the courts to get people put in their care, and they took initiatives to get laws changed in a more humane direction.

Today punishment, and not care, in the community is what is mooted for offenders, and social workers and probation officers are being told that this is what their job must be — to be those punishers in the community. The crisis here is not about what methods or practices to use. It is about the very place of social work values in the scheme of things. The need is to discover a fresh assurance about those values, and a mission based on them.

The Prisoner's Experience

Pet ideas about prisons and prisoners may take a battering when people who are or have been in prison start to talk. What they say may be pretty unpalatable or hard to take, especially if it disturbs cherished notions. Those working in the system, trying to improve it, may find that it is very hard to listen to what may be fierce criticism. It is very easy to dismiss what people in prison say — they're exaggerating; they've got an axe to grind; their case isn't typical. What they say may be an attack on our sense of self-righteousness, our do-gooding, our professional self-esteem. But listen we must. Particularly for the Christian, it is not simply a duty or a charity to visit those in prison — it is an encounter with Jesus, and a final judgment on "religion".

The account which follows is based on a considerable amount of time spent listening. There is already a vast literature on prison from prisoners — in Scotland one only has to think of the writings of Jimmy Boyle, for example. The group included not just prison staff and those familiar with prisons from their work and visitations, but one member who is serving a life sentence. The group visited three Scottish prisons, and spoke to a number of prisoners. We heard from a number of people on our visits. One man gave us a 52 page document, with the Governor's knowledge, setting out his experience. He included a vivid account of riots in one institution, and concluded with his own recommendations and message to the public.

Contradictions

The contradictions and constraints which may be part of the job lot of the various "professionals" — sentencer, psychiatrist, governor, social worker — pale into insignificance in comparison with the experience of the prisoner. "Whether it is the experience of prison, or of imprisonment, or of the whole judicial process, those who have been sentenced to a term of imprisonment would, I believe, agree that if one word can be used to sum up what is meant in this context, that would be 'contradiction'."

"The most obvious contradiction is the perception of the meaning and purpose of punishment. On the one hand, society, and those who are its agents in this matter, claim that it is the loss of liberty that is the punishment. Prisoners, on the other hand, would universally acknowledge that consistent and dehumanising punishment is the inevitable consequence of imprisonment. This *continual* punishment can take many forms, not all of which are obvious to the external observer, or even necessarily to those within the prison system whose task it is to operate it."

The contradiction is therefore very fundamental — it is about the whole meaning and purpose of imprisonment, as seen by the prisoner. Another prisoner wrote: "a casual reader would be encouraged to believe that the Prison Department's *primary* concern is the 're-education' of the offender . . . But the evidence shows that, whether it likes it or not, the Prison Department's first responsibility is *punishment*, the extraction from an offender of a quantified payment (in the currency of time) for an offence. . . . The purpose of the passing of a sentence of imprisonment is firstly that the offender should feel denounced, reviled, *punished*. Any other purpose can be seen only in this context" (Caird, *A Good and Useful Life*, 1974, p. 48). The message here is that the purpose and meaning of prison cannot be discussed separately from society's philosophy and intentions in having prisons, or at least from how that philosophy and intention is experienced by prisoners. The perception is that society is punishing. The experience is that the prisoner does NOT go to prison as the punishment, but that prison is a punishing experience and is an experience of continually being punished.

Slopping Out

"It may seem perfectly in order that a prisoner should be given a pot for toilet facilities when he is locked up. But it is quite another matter to expect that one pot should be shared by two or even three, and that bodily functions of the most private kind should be carried out in the company of others. The level of degradation and loss of intrinsic self-worth involved in this process is *only one indicator* of many other situations in prison life in which the prisoner is made to feel a loss of human dignity, not only in relation to those in authority, but also in relation to his fellow prisoners."

Toilet facilities can become one of the "weapons" if opposition between staff and prisoners becomes the dominant mode. The long account we were given, including a description of a riot, harps on the theme. Whatever the actual circumstances and the intentions of staff, the prisoner's perception is that toilet facilities are denied as part of the staff's need to "control" and "degrade" the prisoner. It is hardly a surprising development that human excrement becomes one of the few "weapons" with which prisoners retaliate. If staff are only to be zoo keepers, it is unlikely to encourage their humanity either.

Petty Tyrannies

"While any one of these dehumanising factors could lead to a perception of imprisonment as continued punishment, it is in conjunction with many other infringements of basic rights that the whole message comes across in no uncertain terms. Overcoming such difficulties is not just a matter of resources, but also one of attitudes on the part of authorities. Being told to take one's ungloved hand out of one's pocket on a freezing cold day is one tiny but symptomatic example. It strengthens the sense of contradiction.

"'When a prisoner reminds those in authority that there exist certain standing orders for their mutual help and protection, he is told not to quote standing orders to staff who are, after all, meant to observe them. This engenders something less than confidence.' The day to day working of the rules is a central factor in underlining the nonsense being made of the rehabilitative ideal. Contradictions arise when staff, who are committed to 'encouraging the prisoner to lead a honest and industrious life' are seen walking out of the gate with a joint of meat under the arm — effectively stealing the prisoner's dinner!"

Another prisoner wrote: "it is these little things which take on a tremendous significance to the inmate, and they mean a great deal in the every day running of the prison. This may be hard for a person on the outside to understand, as they are not faced with filling their time up to the extent that inmates are. If you give prisoners things which are positively orientated and constructive, then the need to refer to that way of thinking (pettiness) will be done away."

Overcrowding

"You get a build up (of risk and tension) in those prisons where many inmates are forced to share a cell designed for one. Quite a number are three to a cell, especially in old, local jails where there is also a lot of coming and going. You must realise the tensions that are created when you are forced to share a cell with one, never mind two, people. You have no option, and the thing is that no one on the face of this earth can get on with everyone that they meet. Imagine what it is like being forced to share a cell for long periods under those conditions — how would you react?"

A professor of criminology makes a similar point: "to talk of 'encouragement to lead a good and useful life' in the context of the present physical and social conditions in many of Britain's prisons is hollow to the point of obscenity." (Bottoms, *The Aims of Imprisonment*, 1990, pp. 1 *et seq*). He quotes, in similar vein: "the spirit of the prison rules is in contradiction to their application. In a prison where physical conditions are similar to those of the Scrubs, it is simply pie-in-the-sky to talk about allowing prisoners to develop their self-respect." One prison governor felt he needed to apologise to prisoners for the conditions in which he had to keep them.

Parole

"The parole policy since 1984 has been point blank . . . there is absolutely nothing to look forward to (if you are serving over 5 years) and no incentive at all to behave because no one else is in the slightest bit interested . . .". And (of the Kincraig Review) "the fact that it is a Lord who is looking into it gives absolutely no confidence to inmates at all, as they are the very same people who . . . battered them with these astronomical sentences in the first place."

Sense of Guilt and Remorse

The suggestion that imprisonment involved a moral process of looking at what one had done, feeling guilt and remorse, met with varied reactions. One lifer emphasised that he was undergoing the pangs of remorse all the time, but that being in prison was irrelevant to that. Most of the others denied any such feelings. One claimed that he was "fitted up"; others regretted getting caught; others again said that they were robbers in the same way that other people were bankers or academics — there was nothing wrong with it.

Help with Problems

"*Large numbers who shouldn't be here*, especially psychiatric cases" was the comment of one group of prisoners. Society, courts, hospitals, can wipe their hands of them. But the prisoners on the hall have to live with people whom they recognise to be disturbed individuals needing a lot of help and not getting it in prison. They felt that the help most people needed was not for the most part forthcoming. Only when numbers were much smaller could there be any hope of people being helped in prison.

At a remand centre for young offenders there was a considerable number of people who are frightened by the whole experience, with some being under constant observation due to suicide risk. A recent study of suicide in prison concluded: "prisons contain an excessive number of people with poor or limited coping skills and it is within this group that are found those that are particularly vulnerable to the effects of stress". It was not simply a case of trying to spot a few individuals at risk so much as "accepting that the prison environment plays an important role in the course of a suicidal crisis." The 8 punishment cells were full at the time of our visit to this institution.

Prisoners put a great emphasis on the need for more education — in a very broad sense. There was great admiration for individuals who came into teach, but there was a feeling that what was needed was a greater emphasis on social education, help with how to fit into society, to feel at home again in an environment which for many was a fearful and strange place. "I saw the need for a help and advice bureau and started to set one up. I set about helping inmates who were coming up to release to organise their problems," wrote the man who gave us the 52 page dossier he had written.

Many prisoners described loneliness and lack of family and friends as a big part of the reason that they were inside. In one sense the prison did at least provide company! But unless something could be done to provide this on the outside, the risk of re-offending would remain.

In another institution there was great praise for the chaplain, whose hours had only recently been increased. The prisoners saw it as useful that he could spend time with them without being part of the establishment. He could also "take the temperature of the place".

Good Things in Prison

The few open and semi-open prisons were much more acceptable than the typical experiences of most mainstream prisons that were being described to us. Staff attitudes in particular were seen as more humane. Where education and training resources were available and being used in these more ordinary prisons, there were again comments of appreciation. The absence of hostility and enmity was notable.

If prisons are run on a militaristic model, the language will be to do with the prisoner as "enemy". The vogue word "targetting" takes on quite a different significance in this context. It is not just a case of punishing prisoners, but of ensuring that they are seen as the "enemy". As enemies they are "non-people", outsiders. See them as people, and the prisoner's experience is that there is then just a possibility of starting to respond in kind.

Central Concerns to the Prisoner

In amongst the detail, some themes emerged time and time again. The sense of contradiction ran through all of them.

"In sum, then, because of the blatant contradictions inherent in the system, and exacerbated by the authorities themselves, the prisoner's experience of prison, while likely to be mixed and to some extent individual, can fairly be said to be that of *abandonment and hopelessness*. No one cares about his plight," was how one prisoner summarised his experience.

"You the public have been demanding and getting longer and longer sentences. You are now beginning to reap the rewards of those policies and wondering why there are so many riots and so forth taking place. It is a well recognised fact, and has been for some time, that prisons only manage to operate on the acceptance and permission of the inmates. If inmates retract their goodwill and acceptance, the situation will get worse, and you need to be realistic and not ignore the signs," warned the prisoner in his 52 page document.

Some prisoners had a very developed sense of injustice. White collar criminals get off scot free. The government is down on drug takers. Parole has been retrospectively abolished. Staff are petty and hypocritical. Prisoners were "wound up", kept apart from their families.

Everyone in one group pointed to the inequalities and social injustices which led many of them into crime in the first place. They pointed to lack of decent jobs, decent houses, decent schools and neighbourhoods. Law-abiding morality was something one couldn't *afford* in the kind of situations they had experienced.

The Meaning of Imprisonment

The prisoner's experience is that imprisonment is a contradiction. At a recent conference Bishop David Jenkins reflected on it this way (*The Meaning of Imprisonment*, 1990, p. 46 *et seq*):

> "The meaning of imprisonment is that our society dumps its legally defined failures and nuisances on people who run custodial establishments. The people who are dumped are so dumped because they have legally and judicially been declared to be responsible for, and so guilty of, those disturbing, damaging, and troubling acts which have come to be defined and declared as 'crimes'. The Prison Service, on whom they are dumped, does not really know what to do with them, largely because it has never been made really and sufficiently clear what they are expected to do with them. In any case, whatever is expected, the means for providing it have not been sufficiently provided.
>
> "Our prisons are a disgrace — not a disgrace to the Prison Service, *but to us* — the public, or citizens, or what you will. The disgrace arises from what we, through Parliament and the institutions set up by departments of state or other bodies responsible to Parliament, support, condone, or ignore in institutions which are maintained to deal with a certain class or classes of people who trouble us, disturb our peace, or cause us un-ease, dis-ease, damage, and fear."

In a word, the disgrace has to do with us, as much, if not more than, with the prisoner.

Part 2

REFLECTION

I
The Vacuum in Penal Policy

The End of Rehabilitation

The crisis in the criminal justice system with which this book is concerned is the uncertainty over aims and values in the wake of the collapse of the rehabilitative ideal. Aims associated with this ideal, and the idea of "treatment", held sway for decades. However, the system of thought around this ideal is now out of favour, and a vacuum has been created. Practitioners in the penal system struggle in their various spheres to operate humane values, but feel oppressed by an emphasis on punishment and justice which does not satisfy their sense of vocation and purpose. We have also seen the consequences of the emphasis on punishment for the prisoner. We believe also that such an emphasis on punishment alone makes for an unhealthy society.

What was the Rehabilitative Ideal?

The rehabilitative ideal was an ideology — a whole framework of ideas and objectives. Fitful instances of reform and of attempts to deal humanely with people in trouble can be found in the history of penal matters, but the publication of the Gladstone Report in 1895 is often seen as the start of more systematic attempts to lessen the rigours of punishment and to seek to reform offenders. Instead of concentrating on past evil done and the moral weaknesses of the evil-doer, the focus was to be on moral improvement, training, and turning out a better person and citizen as the result of the system's efforts.

Changes and improvements within prisons did occur, and non-custodial measures, such as probation, were developed;

a system of after-care became an integral part of some of the new sentences such as Borstal Training. A whole series of supporting ideologies and languages lay behind these various rehabilitative measures. There was a sense of optimism about these new approaches, and an important sense of doing something positive, which informed the consciousness of those in the system and their attitude towards offenders.

Along with advocacy for reform, the emergent social and psychological sciences were influential. They supplied, as it were, a theoretical support for the ideals of reformers, by providing a "Treatment Model". Ordinarily "treatment" means simply what is done to someone. In the context of the rehabilitative ideal, the treatment model was a coherent and logically elaborated system of thought. It meant a lot more than specific "treatments", such as probation or borstal.

As a body of thought, the treatment approach had remarkable rhetorical power and commanded enormous influence. It presented itself as a rational, scientific alternative to punishment. It had a comprehensive, totalising character — able to explain everything. It was regarded as similar to clinical medicine. Crime and criminals could be "treated". The important notions were — pathology, causation, and cures. These needed investigation, expert assessment and diagnosis. Then you applied the appropriate individualised treatment, and left it to the experts to decide when it had "worked".

The treatment approach made converts of those who had advocated philanthropic and charitable approaches to penal reform. Their case had been a primarily moral one. The new model overtook this with its own distinctively "high-tec" version, drawing on all the prestige of science and the medical profession. It was not "soft" but based on the tough-mindedness of science. It promised the best of all worlds — a humane, scientific approach which would cure individuals *and* reduce crime.

The approach conquered the hearts and minds of social workers, probation officers, and some prison governors — and so too did the professional claims and status that went with it. It became part of policy.

The Treatment Model in Practice

As usual, practice was not quite so logical, nor did it fit into a coherent theory. Rather, it was a patchwork of compromise and contradiction, which combined these new ideas and approaches with older, more punitive attitudes, and many institutions which remained unreformed and inhumane. Much of it remains so today. But the language of treatment began to become "official". New procedures were introduced, such as reports to the court before sentence, which were based on the ideas of investigation and assessment. Specialised institutions claiming rehabilitative régimes were set up. Indeterminate sentences were introduced and seen as a means of giving "treatment" time to work. Some authority was attributed to various experts — prison governors, social workers, psychiatrists — based on their scientific training and expertise.

Most of what was called treatment was actually social work in its various forms. Only a minority of offenders received anything like full therapeutic treatment of the kind that the "theory" might suggest. While social work thought of itself in treatment forms, it doesn't for the most part quite fit the full "medical model". Most of what was offered was more mundane — counselling, support, assistance and advice. *It may have been no less valuable for all that.*

Treatment in practice was modest, infrequent, and better described simply as training, education, or social work supervision and help. *The majority of offenders, who were fined, or put in local prisons for short sentences, never received anything remotely approaching "treatment".*

Weaknesses of the Treatment Model

In more recent years both the treatment approach and the theories underpinning it have come in for serious criticism. A whole catalogue of criticism has emerged which has led most academics and practitioners to reject the treatment model as "theoretically faulty, systematically discriminatory, and inconsistent with some of our most basic concepts of justice" (American Friends Service Committee, *Struggle for Justice*, 1971 p. 12).

The most telling points have been:

1 That the theory on which the treatment model is based is an inadequate explanation of crime. There are many social and environmental factors which contribute to crime, and yet the treatment model focusses only upon the individual and his or her "maladjustment".

2 That the the approach can be oppressive, arbitrary and manipulative:

   a) a focus on a person's "needs" rather than their "deeds", forgets that people should be punished for something they have done, not for being the kinds of people they are; the focus could neglect concern with guilt in favour of issues of normality and acceptability;
   b) although "welfare" can be helpful, it can also involve a kind of tyranny: people were sometimes forced into a particular kind of "cure" that was decided as being right for them, without reference to their own ideas; individuals were thus denied the respect accorded to rational, responsible people;
   c) people could end up being detained longer than their original offence justified, on the basis that their "treatment" had not been given enough time to "work";
   d) it was a discretionary system that could often impose middle class values of socialisation and therapy on people who did not share those values or the culture associated with them.

3 Whilst the treatment approach was seen as positive, utilitarian, and efficacious as against old-fashioned harmful and irrational punishment, it had little explicit concern with moral values and moral argument. In place of the moral and religious concerns of the earlier reformers, there was simply an amoral promise of technical achievement.

4 *It didn't work.* A large research literature showed that claims for the efficiency of treatment measures — conceived of in terms of reducing subsequent offending — were not in fact well founded. Most treatment régimes failed to reform their "clients", and, in this respect, were little better than traditional non-treatment régimes.

Having originally moved ground from a moral case to a technical one, and basing its promise on scientific assurance that it could "deliver", the failure to cure criminals or reduce crime was the model's death-knell.

The Need for a Debate about Values

Now that the all-encompassing treatment model has fallen from its pedestal, two kinds of problems are left.

First, practitioners may be confused and/or directionless in their work. They are dissatisfied with any idea of simply returning to the old legal principles of sentencing, and ideas of retribution and just deserts. People are left going through the motions, becoming cynical, and with feelings that vary between routine low-morale and occasional identity-crisis. Individuals are left struggling to find ideas and justifications which make sense of what they are doing, in the face of social and political emphases which stress the more negative and punitive side of the penal system.

Second, there is a need to establish new goals and expectations for the criminal justice system. The lessons of the model's failure need to be learned. What has been discredited is the general claim that treatment works and should be the central aim of the system, not so much that specific treatments have no value. *It is a model and its premises that are to be rejected, not necessarily the ideals of offering help, services, opportunities, or even "treatments" to people who get caught up in the system.*

The virtues of charity, care, help, training, and hope have not been shown to be invalid. Rather they have been brought into disrepute by their association with the treatment approach. Now that their influence in the penal system can't be justified on the grounds of crime reduction, some other basis for their adoption is required.

What has appeared to have feet of clay, therefore, is the treatment model, in the sense of a particular set of theories and techniques claiming to explain everything and to prevent crime. The collapse of this model exposes us to the moral debate about the values which should be operative in our criminal justice system. There is no consensus any more, if there ever was one, that the system should have the welfare of offenders as its aim.

In the larger social and political sphere there has also been a collapse of the "welfare consensus" (See, Morris, *Consensus versus Ideology*, 1990, for example). In that setting, alternative ideas such as "market forces", "individual responsibility" and so on are being emphasised. In criminal justice, the idea of punishment is being pushed to the fore, so that imprisonment is once again being seen by many as a punishment, and nothing more, and even social work is being redefined as "punishment in the community".

The Emergence of the Justice Model

Introduction

In the wake of the collapse of the "rehabilitative ideal" there has been a growing emphasis on a so-called "Justice Model". Critics of the treatment approach complained that however humane and progressive its intentions, it could lead to injustice. People have looked to a "justice model" to provide a basis for penal policy to replace the rehabilitative ideal. The idea has been that, if we are unable to "do good" through punishment, we can at least "do justice". Thus, it is suggested, the aims of the system should be nothing more than ensuring that every offender gets his or her just deserts, no more and no less.

Reflection on this justice model left us with a feeling of dissatisfaction. No doubt this kind of formal justice is a necessary and important element of any fair system, but it did not seem to us to be a sufficient basis upon which to deal with the lives of those in institutions or under supervision. Nor was it clear what was meant by its key term "justice". It did not appear to meet sufficiently the needs of practitioners for a sense of purpose, the needs that people in trouble have, or, we would argue, the needs of society. It was from this position — that the justice model did not fill the vacuum left by the collapse of the rehabilitative ideal — that our search turned to theology and Christian belief, in order to explore what concept of justice might emerge from that quarter.

Critique of Rehabilitation

As noted above, criticism of the rehabilitative ideal included not simply arguments about faulty theory, or even lack of success, but the crucial ground that it could lead to injustice. The complaints from a "justice" perspective fastened on to aspects such as:

a) the treatment model dealt with an offence as a symptom of something else rather than as a matter in its own right, and thus played down issues of guilt and responsibility;
b) the aspect of indeterminacy in many sentences (including non-custodial ones), and the dangers of excessive discretion which this allowed;
c) the facts that discretionary decision making could not be judicially challenged (particularly in relation to parole, for example), that it was secret, and that the criteria were unclear and unstated;
d) it exacerbated the social and other disadvantages of many people who came into the system, in that they could be detained longer or experience levels of intervention arising from their social circumstances, and not from their crime; it became an extension of social control and oppression of the poor;
e) punishment should fit the crime, not the criminal; society has a right to respond to the wrongs that people commit and the harm they inflict upon each other and on society, but not the right to demand that they should be of a particular personality type.

Elements of the Justice Model

As with rehabilitation, there are a number of ideologies and languages supporting various elements in a "justice" model. Advocates of the various elements have their own wider agendas and frames of reference.

1   Emphasis on Rights and "Due Process"

This emphasis challenged the grandiose claims advanced for rehabilitation, but sought to avoid any return to harsh and oppressive punishments. It was concerned to see people treated well and humanely, but equally that their rights should be explicitly stated and observed. One expression of this emphasis was the idea that prisons should only aim for "humane containment", which we met in part one. There is a degree of realism in this idea. It reflects the reality of experience — that few prisoners actually get "treatment", and that many prisons are not even resourced to maintain humane standards. It also aimed to include remand prisoners within its compass, which the "good and useful life" formula did not.

It was felt, however, to lack any sense of purpose in dealing with people. You don't have to do anything with anyone. It was simply warehousing — albeit hopefully now humane warehousing. The May Committee felt this and suggested "positive custody" as a concept that avoided the language of treatment but kept some of its sense of purpose. However this too was an ill-defined aim, and in the years since 1979 has not led to a notable improvement in prison conditions of itself, nor provided any particular sense of mission or purpose.

2   Return to Punishment, Deterrence, and Incapacitation

This strand picked up the complaint that the rehabilitative ideal did not treat the business of crime sufficiently seriously.

The concern now was to see that punishment should be an effective deterrent, and that it should protect the public effectively. Rehabilitation was flawed because it sought to shift the penal system away from punishment itself. It was also seen as focussing excessively on the offender, and as overlooking innocent victims or innocent society.

This view reflects moral stances and views about individual behaviour which are in sharp contrast with the insights of the social and psychological sciences that underpinned the rehabilitative ideal, and the moral concerns of reformers. It stresses individual responsibility virtually to the exclusion of any social factors and environmental factors which influence the commission of crime. It appears to allow no place for social concern for those in trouble — even suggesting, at times, that there is no such thing as society.

However, this view also has to take on board the evidence that the system is not very good at deterrence and incapacitation. The view often persists in the teeth of this evidence.

This approach to "justice" has little in common with the concerns for rights and realism described above — concerns raised equally in the name of "justice".

3   Just Deserts

This argument emphasises the issue of guilt as the only justification for punishment, and stresses issues of the individual's morality. The approach replaces the treatment model's view of the individual as "patient" or in some way "ill" and replaces it with an emphasis on the moral responsibility and rational choice of the individual offender. Its focus is on the acts that offenders have committed, the guilt element in them, and the proportionality of the punishment to those acts and that guilt. It does seek to avoid institutionalising retaliation, and brutalising the offender. It does seek to deal with the offender as a moral agent.

However, like the rehabilitative ideal, its focus is on individuals, almost in isolation. It looks backward to the offence, but lacks any of the hope of the rehabilitationist as an element in the punishment to be imposed. It is concerned only to allocate retributive punishment in respect of that offence, and offers no positive or constructive vision for rebuilding damaged social relationships or helping the offender towards self-improvement.

Weaknesses of the Justice Model

The justice model may have served to point up elements that are missing in the rehabilitative ideal, but it does not of itself appear to provide an adequate philosophy for criminal justice. It has drawn attention to issues of guilt; of people's rights and the need for humane conditions; and to moral considerations in offending and justice. But in its turn, it has a number of deficiencies that suggest to us that *a larger concept of justice is needed* than that offered by this model, or the points made in its name.

There are three areas of weakness:

1 It tends to narrow legalistic and formal approaches. "Doing justice" becomes merely following and applying rules, without concern about the merits of the case, or the social and human issues which are involved. It takes law as expressing a given consensus within society, whereas some laws may reflect the views and power of only certain sections of society; and where the administration of even those laws about which agreement is more general is discriminatory and socially unjust.

2 It is backward looking, insufficiently purposeful and literally "hopeless". It does not motivate or put fire in the belly of practitioners. The focus on acts and guilt that it introduces simply goes back to the deed and responds to it arithmetically and non-relationally. There is no looking at the issues that may be behind the deed, or the human relationships that may be damaged as a result of it. It still leaves out victims, except possibly in some financial ways. It leaves out "society", in the sense that it contributes little to the improvement of civil life or the affirmation of humane social values.

3 It is based on a hopelessly limited view of the individual and society. Its premise of individuals as moral equals, and rational agents, is pure fantasy when confronted with the reality of social disadvantage, personal need, and emotional inadequacy that is the real experience of people who get caught up in the system.

The narrow legalism, backward looking focus, fictional equality, and view of the human condition on which the justice model is based make it a hopelessly inadequate basis for criminal justice policy.

II
A Theological Perspective

The Role of Theology in the Debate

If there is a vacuum in penal policy because a particular approach has fallen from grace, or a replacement model is inadequate, it may be tempting to look to Christianity or to theology for some kind of immediate answer or solution to fill that gap. People may look to theology for an alternative model or theory to explain everything, and to give a sense of purpose and direction that is missing.

The first problem is that theology is a minority interest. We live in a secular pluralist society, in which there is a great diversity of beliefs and values: there is no one shared view of the world. However much it may be argued that this is a Christian country in some formal, official, or outward respects, church goers are only about 10% of the population. There are even different beliefs and theologies within the Christian tradition. Moreover there is nowadays a greater diversity of religious groups in our society, not necessarily sharing any Christian beliefs. So simply giving some kind of in-house doctrinal exposition is not going to help people who do not share that particular frame of reference.

A second problem, associated with this, is that people generally do not interpret their experience in the light of religious kinds of explanations. They may well not be familiar with basic Christian beliefs and doctrines, even if they have some kind of soft spot for religion, or some vague memories from childhood of biblical stories. Indeed they may have half-baked kinds of religious ideas which would make a theologian shudder. They may dress up natural or ordinary feelings of punitiveness in quasi-religious guise,

67

without necessarily being aware of what religion may really want to be saying on the issue. It has to be said that some Christians fall into the same or similar traps.

A third problem is that there is a danger in theology offering itself as some kind of substitute theory to explain the world and produce a specific plan of action. Theology can fall into the same trap as any other theory — that facts are made to fit the theory rather than vice versa. Moreover a theory which starts off as an attempt to try and explain something, can end up by becoming a rule for conduct. Given the confusion and the variety of "models" that we have come across in the penal system, it is a natural temptation to look to Christianity to provide an "explanation" for all the behaviour for which other theories may now be found wanting. It is also tempting to look to it to provide a blueprint for the kind of approach that should now be adopted.

When theology has attempted to be a kind of theory that comes from outside a situation, to give tidy explanations, and to tell people what they ought to do, it has usually ended up either mystifying the situation, or as justifying what is really a quite unacceptable situation. The record of the churches and of Christians in supporting the unacceptable is notorious: it may in part be the result of this kind of theology. It has a lot of which to repent in the way it has propped up some unacceptable parts of the penal system over the years.

The aim of the theological exploration undertaken in the group which wrote this book was, first of all, to listen to those who had experience of the criminal justice system, and to see what problems, frustrations, and sense of vocation emerged from their involvement in practice. The second task was to see what biblical ideas and Christian beliefs appeared to bear on the issues and themes which emerged. Practitioners responded to various stories and values suggested in the Bible as more or less relevant to their experience and vocation. Concepts such as guilt which were part of their everyday working were tested against biblical understandings. In turn, emphases and ideas from the Bible were considered as possible alternative values that could shed light on problems in criminal justice.

Whilst Christian beliefs may be those of a minority in Britain today, if they express truths which are in any sense public and important, and which commend themselves to others working in the system, and to society at large, then they deserve to be taken seriously.

From the tradition of liberation theology, people are discovering afresh that they learn about God in practical commitment, in the experience of oppression, and in trying to change things for the better. Indeed we discovered in part one that it wasn't just people like victims and prisoners who were experiencing oppression, as might initially be expected, but also that people working in the system were feeling oppressed by factors such as prison conditions, political pressures, and unsympathetic public opinion.

Theology looks at this kind of practical experience, reviews it in the light of the best kinds of social analysis available, and tests it out in a dialogue with the Bible and with Christian tradition. Theology does not try to become a theory, or a mould into which experience, practice, and structures must be forced. Rather it tries to be a lamp on the way, a help to those who are struggling to fulfil their vocations. What theology finds is that tidy certainties get disturbed! Again and again typical ideas and approaches were challenged by theology, and new ways of looking at issues suggested. There was a sense of excitement about some of the ideas, as well as a wariness about the consequences that would follow from taking them seriously.

Is there a Theology of Punishment?

Justifying Punishment

To punish means to cause suffering. Many books have been written, and arguments been raised, about the possible justifications for punishment. Because punishment is unpleasant, because it is uncomfortable, society needs to feel that it is justified. Is there a possible theological justification for punishment?

There is a whole repertoire of words and ideas associated

with justifications for punishment. Deterring the offender; deterring other potential offenders; denouncing the behaviour in question; asserting social standards; cleansing the offender; causing the offender to suffer proportionately to the damage caused; and even rehabilitating the offender.

A basic problem in the criminal justice system is that there are several quite different understandings of punishment and its rationale at work. They are often not compatible with one another. In such a confusing situation ideologies and even "theologies" can seem to give respectability to a system which is full of anomalies, conflicts, and inhumanity. Only when there is greater clarity about what is meant by punishment and what it is intended to effect, is it possible to consider the possibility of theological validation.

The reality of punishment in our experience of the criminal justice system is that:

— it does not deter effectively;
— it antagonises offenders and excludes them from society;
— it creates scapegoats, and bonds society together against offenders;
— it often hinders offenders from confronting their offending effectively;
— instead it forces them to deal with the punishment inflicted upon them;
— it may encourage the baser instincts of society;
— it creates feelings of frustration, anger, and humiliation in offenders;

Whatever the philosophical or legal or moral cases that can be advanced for punishment, we have found that the criminal justice system is in fact a system of social control, heavily punitive, and very concerned with blaming, scapegoating, and exclusion. Much punishment is about maintaining boundaries between "us" and "them" — criminals, dangerous offenders, or whatever. The wrath of the community is visited upon the wrong-doer. All these themes can be found in the Bible. It is possible to quote scripture selectively in support of all kinds of causes. The Devil himself is reported as quoting scripture as a tempting justification for a proposed course of action (Matthew, 4:1-10).

The most important thing to notice, however, is that a dominant *theme* in the New Testament is that Jesus has taken all the blame upon himself, and has absorbed it. Any condemnation is cancelled. Those who follow in the ways of Jesus should accept this. The emphasis shifts to the issue of following Jesus and the discipline involved.

Discipline as a Possible Context for Punishment

Discipline is another of those words that does not necessarily have the best of associations. The main grade officers in prisons are called the "discipline officers". The word can easily call up military and authoritarian ideas and pictures in the mind. Discipline is another of those words that may need to be "rehabilitated".

The root of the word discipline means "learning" — the same root as for "disciple". It is better, to start with, if we think of discipline within an educational frame of reference. The person disciplined should learn and grow through the process. Discipline is for disciples — i.e. people who are following a way or a person, rather than obeying a law.

Through discipline people are brought back into fellowship and held within it. Through discipline in a context which is just, fair, and loving, the offender's worth and responsibility and potentiality are recognised and affirmed. Punishment is the negative side of a comprehensive process of growth in which both positive and negative incentives may have their part to play. But punishment outwith that context, punishment that is only one-sided and without that greater purpose, would be unjust.

Discipline is not regimentation, or the infliction of pain geared to the needs of the inflicters. It is rather the support for a structure of relationships in which people can grow and develop. This is not to say that discipline is pleasant or easy. Even an academic or educational discipline is hard, painful, or difficult. But it is undertaken because a purpose or goal for the study and the acceptance of rules, teachers, and work can be seen by the learner. Growth can be fastest at a time of crisis — such as a mistake. That is a time of opportunity, of the possibility of leaping to a new level of learning.

It is sometimes suggested that Scotland is a punitive society because of the influence of Calvinism. The following quotation from the old Calvinist form of discipline may therefore come as something of a surprise. Here discipline speaks of solidarity in offence and in forgiveness (Calvin, *Church Discipline*, 1571).

> "We in the sin of this our brother accuse and condemn our own sins, in his fall we all lament and consider our sinful nature, also we shall join repentance, tears and prayers with him and his, knowing that no flesh can be justified before God's presence, if judgment proceed without mercy . . . We all here present join our sins with your sin; we all repute and esteem your fall to be our own; we accuse ourselves no less than you; and now, finally, we join our prayers with yours, that we and you may obtain mercy, and that by the means of our Lord Jesus Christ."

Discipline looks to the future, to forgiveness, and through that to the hope of something better to come. Discipline without forgiveness is brutal: forgiveness without discipline is cheap. Forgiveness is not the ignoring of the offence, or pretending that it never happened. But it is the expunging of an offence, following on recognition of its gravity. Forgiveness is primarily God's, and is shown supremely on the cross. Our forgiving of others — of our "debtors", as the Scottish form of the Lord's prayer has it — is a response to God's forgiveness of us. Secular talk of "paying one's debt" needs to be seen in this context.

So in this section we shall lay the ground for an answer to the question posed by our title. Forgiveness is the end of punishment. *Only forgiveness can provide a theological justification and a purpose for punishment.*

God's Response to Wrong-doing

At the heart of the Christian tradition we find a radical critique of the concept of punishment. Offences are clearly recognised and condemned as sin. But the *response* to them offers something quite new.

Christian experience shows that God's response to human misdeeds:

— does not require suffering or pain as a condition for acceptance;
— does not demand retaliation;
— does not condemn or exclude the offender;
— does not primarily aim to express divine wrath.

Instead, God:

— accepts the offender without condoning the offence;
— requires the offender to face up to the reality of that offence;
— invites the offender into a community of reconciliation;
— encourages the offender to lead life with a new attitude;
— declares the offender to be free from the offence;
— invites the person to follow in service as a "disciple".

The idea of discipline/discipleship as education and up-bringing carries with it the idea of looking towards the fulfilment of adulthood and maturity. It looks forward, not back at past offences.

In the Bible the life of discipleship is compared to a race (Hebrews, 12:1, *et seq*). We have to undergo the discipline of training, sometimes hard training, towards the end of running the race. The runners look to Jesus who has already undergone the discipline/hardship of the cross — for the sake of the joy that lay before him. Hardships can be taken on board as an aspect of training in the life of faith. In them we can experience sure signs of God's care for us. His discipline is not arbitrary, but arises out of his care for us. A loving family without discipline is inconceivable. But a family in which there is much punishment, or punishment in lieu of care, is one which has become unloving and unjust.

God's justice is not "fair" in human terms. It is more than fair — it goes beyond ideas of fairness within our human "justice models". There is a story Jesus told about a number of labourers taken on at different times of the one day, but who all receive the same payment at the end of the day, however much work they have done. It is not a lesson in Christian economics. It is an affirmation that people are treated without regard to their work, to their achievement, or to the degree that they may be "deserving". All equally are valued and accepted totally. God's justice cannot be calculated arithmetically, or by criteria of "proportionality" so beloved of our legal system. It is a creative justice — looking to create something new from the brokenness resulting from offending.

Divine Justice

The roles of offender and judge are two central ones in the criminal justice system. In our description of people's experience of the system, we began with the judge, and ended with the offender. The system of criminal justice distinguishes the "guilty" from the "innocent", and then the innocent inflict a penalty on the guilty. The guilty "deserves" the penalty for his or her misdeeds. That is how most people understand the process.

Christian belief disturbs this formulation, and turns it on its head. We might expect to start with the idea of God as Judge, and examine his reaction to people's misdeeds. What we in fact find when we do this is that his reaction to those misdeeds is to enter our system in human form, as Jesus of Nazareth. Moreover the culmination of the story is that Jesus is convicted of crime and labelled as offender. Without "deserving" it, he suffers the extreme penalty of the criminal law. God, who is indeed the Judge, is designated as an offender in a human system.

The Judge as Offender and the Offender as Judge

There are some important points to draw out from the story of the Incarnation — God coming into the world in human form. The main one is that God identifies himself with humanity: he knows what it is to be human. But of particular relevance is his identification, very clearly in the story of his birth, for example, with the poor and the oppressed — the *very sections of society from which most of those whom we prosecute in our system come*. In the story of the sheep and the goats, to give another example, we are told that we meet

Jesus in feeding the hungry, clothing the naked, and *visiting the prisoner* (Matthew, 25:31–46).

The story of Jesus begins with his being placed with the poor and the oppressed. It ends with his trial on criminal charges. Jesus is convicted of the most serious offences — of blasphemy by the religious authorities, and of treason by the secular authority. He is declared by authority to be an offender. He experiences arrest, abuse, torture, and briefly imprisonment, before experiencing the ultimate penalty — death, by crucifixion. In the vernacular of today one could say, "he was framed" — trumped up charges, false evidence, pressure from "rent-a-crowd" public opinion. He did indeed "take the rap".

The judge in this story, in one sense, was Pilate. The way history will remember him probably doesn't do the profession of being a judge much good in the general mind. His judgment and verdict were based not so much on seeking to establish truth and justice, as on expediency and convenience.

The religious authorities, equally, could not cope with a view of God which did not fit their own self-interest and prejudice, and they made their judgments accordingly.

From a Christian perspective, God, in the form of Jesus, *remains the judge in this story*. The story represents a challenge to our human understanding of judges and judging. The story highlights the danger in any judicial process that compromise and prejudice can "crucify" the offender. In very important senses, *the offender is our judge. And the way we treat offenders is a judgment on our society*.

The Aim of Divine Justice

There is a much larger purpose to all this than merely holding up a mirror to human criminal justice systems. Jesus is cast in the role of offender for the *very sake of those who reject and condemn him*. God deals with those who do him wrong by putting himself in their position and bearing the penalty for them. This is a complete reversal of our human ideas about punishment. God, the only one entitled to punish, takes the punishment on himself. The experience of

Christians is that, though we can in no way avoid the consequences of our own wrong-doing, we have to confront and accept our wrongness; but that we do not have to pay the penalty for it, because it has already been paid for us.

In this frame of reference, *we are all offenders*; none of us is innocent and thus entitled to punish. Our guilt can only be dealt with by the innocent one we have offended forgiving us *and* bearing our penalty for us. This in turn conditions our approach to the wrong-doing of others. We can only ask "forgive us our trespasses", if we are prepared to "forgive those who trespass against us".

In Christian belief, the judgment of the cross is resolved and vindicated in the event of the resurrection and exaltation of Jesus. The crucified/offender is raised to God's presence. That in turn opens access to God for those on whose behalf he pleads. In this respect He is described in the Bible as "our only Mediator and Advocate" — a combination of roles that in our system we would ordinarily consider to be rather separate and different.

A final important point of Christian belief here is that the forgiveness of God is available to all; as a result of what Jesus has accomplished, access to God is open to all.

The Nature of the Judge

We have various ideas of what a judge is or should be. We have various expectations of them in our society. We saw in part one that they are not encouraged to discuss their job with others outside their own circle.

At the centre of Christian belief there is an inversion of the roles of judge and offender that upsets our ordinary kinds of formulations. What sort of a judge is God?

There is a picture in the Bible of God both as judge and as law-giver. This picture is found mainly in the Old Testament section of the Bible, but it has a number of important points to contribute to our discussion.

The laws that God makes are viewed here as an expression or manifestation of his character — that he is holy, that he cares for creation, and provides for his people. The various facets of the law are seen as expressing his intention that people should live together in harmony and relationship, and in obedience to the laws. Law is something in which to delight.

The law is seen not only as being a set of demands, but also as a gift to the community. Human justice is expected to follow the pattern set by the law which, in its turn, expresses the character and intention of God. Human agents of justice are expected at all times to be the agents of God's justice thus revealed.

There is a telling story about King David in this connection. The prophet Nathan tells him a story about a man taking another man's lamb. David is getting all self-righteous and ready to inflict punishment and justice, when Nathan says to him, "You are the man!", for David was doing precisely the same thing (II Samuel, 12:1, *et seq*). David judges himself in the light of the story told by Nathan, and the incident is part of his growth and education.

A central attribute of God that crops up time and time again is his "righteousness" — not a word used often in everyday parlance. This quality of God has two aspects to it. At one and the same time it demands punishment and reparation for wrong-doing, *but without separating this from mercy and love*. It looks to the offender being restored into relationship and into the community.

Human laws are just only in so far as they too participate in this characteristic of righteousness — that is, *they include the virtues of mercy and love*. The laws of Israel set out in the Old Testament provide for order, respect, and mercy within the community. The criminal law gave particular attention to restitution and the limitation of vengeance.

Moreover, God's righteousness is not seen as an unattractive, cold, distant quality, but rather as involving a specially close and loving relationship with the community. It is a relationship of mutual commitment and responsibility. God undertakes to sustain the community, he seeks to hold the community in relationship with him. He is described as constantly seeking to guide that community and to restore it to him when it goes astray. A very evocative illustration of this can be found in the book of Hosea, for example: from the experience of himself being married to a prostitute and constantly forgiving her, in his love for her, for her repeated infidelities, Hosea provides an insight into the forgiving nature of God.

The Law of Love

The New Testament shares with the Old the understanding that God's grace undergirds all law, and that the law's chief function is to bring about relations of love and respect in human relationships, and between humans and God. The emphasis on love in Jesus' teaching does not invalidate the emphases of the Old Testament. Jesus reinforced the law in his teaching. He described his mission as being to fulfil the law and the prophets. He re-interpreted the law in the spirit of love.

Jesus wanted to see the law of love obeyed rather than mere obedience to a set of statutes. In the story of the prodigal son, the father's love forgave the penitent son, and marked his return with a feast (Luke, 15:11, *et seq*). The self-righteous obedient legalism of the elder brother is pictured as less attractive. There are other examples of strict obedience to the minutiae of statute as being of secondary priority in comparison with other objectives — for example, healing on the Sabbath was more important than obeying the precise letter of a particular law (Luke, 10:13, *et seq*).

The secular law of today clearly does not have the purpose of expressing the characteristics of God as holy and righteous. However, roles such as enabling moral values to be expressed in the ordering and structure of the community may be seen as some reflection of biblical ideas. Any inclusion within the law of protection for the weak and disadvantaged certainly echoes biblical emphases. These echoes can be seen as a partial expression of values important from a Christian perspective.

However some much stronger points can be drawn from this perspective to be set against aspects of our current ways of thinking in criminal justice. A central theme is that punishment and reparation, if they are to have a place, should go together with mercy and love. Another emphasis here that is rare in our own times is that the aim of the law should be to restore relationships and bring people back into the community. Of the greatest importance, from a Christian point of view, is the emphasis of Jesus on the law of love.

Possibly the most telling story in the New Testament bearing on our concern with offending and punishment is that of the woman caught in adultery (John 7:53, *et seq*). The woman was brought to Jesus and there was no doubt as to her guilt; the penalty appears to have been death by stoning. The response to her offending — underlining a point that recurs throughout this section on theological exploration—was Jesus' remark, "let him that is without sin cast the first stone".

It is also worth bearing in mind another teaching of Jesus to the effect that you do not necessarily have to do the deed to be as good as guilty: he spoke on another occasion of man "already having committed adultery with her in his heart" (Matthew, 5:28). *So the standard Jesus sets of what is wrong is a very high one, but there is an even higher standard about the right to punish.*

In the story about the woman, no one did cast the first stone. But the story did not finish there. There is no question of Jesus undermining either the law or questioning the prescribed penalty. He affirms the law, but does not condemn the offender. He simply says, "go and sin no more". Justice and forgiveness are intended to lead to a change of life style! That is the nature of divine justice.

Human Justice and Divine Justice

Most systems of criminal justice are forms of social control, heavily punitive, concerned with blaming, scapegoating, and exclusion. Much punishment is about boundary maintenance, not about personal conversion or social transformation. Justice today is a contested concept — there are many conflicting notions of what justice is. These various under-standings can be used to support various kind of penal policy. For instance, some models of justice look back to the offence and try to calculate the "just deserts" of the offender and adjust the penalty accordingly. Other models, such as rehabilitation, concentrate on the person and look to the future, but carry within their ideologies dangers of injustice of different kinds.

There is thus a muddle about justice. As a consequence penal policy operates in a moral vacuum. In such a situation there is a particular danger that concepts of justice may be used and manipulated so that they serve sectional interests, typically of dominant groups in society.

Christians affirm that God is just and loving. Christians experience true justice in God's dealings with them, finding that mercy and love are at the heart of God's justice. God's justice is for our good, even though it often disturbs our ideas and our behaviour. Our behaviour should exemplify and pass on that kind of justice, mercy, and love.

God's justice does not just challenge people at an individual level. It challenges classical and conventional accounts of justice as fairness, or giving each his or her due.

God's justice is more than fair. *It is a creative rather than an arithmetical fairness*. Justice as arithmetical fairness is a compromise — an approximation only to the mercy and love which lie at the heart of God's justice.

Another tradition within Christianity reflects this problem of the wide gap between human justice systems and the ideals suggested by God's justice. This tradition sees human criminal justice systems as a defence against sin. This way of thinking does remind us of the gravity and the power of sin and evil and offending: it warns against too sunny an account of human character and behaviour. Only the justice of God's kingdom can give the authentic flavour of justice to the human systems of this world. Without this frame of reference, human systems of criminal justice become hard, mechanical and unforgiving — as our system has largely become.

There is a need therefore for a model of God's justice to be visible. The church, as a preliminary and partial manifestation of God's kingdom, should exemplify in its behaviour, its procedures, and its structures, the justice of God. It should assess human systems of criminal justice in the light of its knowledge and experience of the justice, mercy, and love of God. It is not just that the church should speak out. By its very being it should witness to the justice of God. It should be the example and the light so that others can see that divine justice.

Forgiveness and Reconciliation

All are Offenders

There are no innocent human beings, according to the teaching of the New Testament. There is a basic human solidarity in sin, offence, and guilt. We are all offenders (Romans, 3:23).

This seems to make nonsense of ordinary understandings. It is patently not true that everyone has committed criminal offences. It does not seem a helpful idea to suggest that law abiding people are the same as those who have broken the law, or been prosecuted. It is not an idea necessarily calculated to make people feel at one with them, or sympathetic towards them.

Even from a secular perspective a number of points can be made. One is that there are a number of double standards in relation to crime: attitudes to serious traffic offences, the differentiation between alcohol and other drugs, are among illustrations that could be given. Perhaps more importantly, attention can be drawn to differential practices in relation to those who are prosecuted by the criminal justice system. A great proportion of those prosecuted are young men aged between 17 and 25 from the "lower social classes" on the Registrar General's classification system. Yet similar behaviour by others (e.g. "white collar crime", "institutional crime") can be treated very differently. If the point were to be expressed in quasi-religious language, the saying "there but for the grace of God go I" might come to mind. In the criminal justice context an adaptation might be suggested — "there but for social class and the grace of God go I".

From a Christian perspective other things are also being said — though the perspective would include a critique of any double standards or hypocrisy, or social injustice. The

Christian perspective would point to motivation, as well as to actual deeds, even if the inner motivation is known only to God. It would also point to the fact that all break God's laws, even if all do not transgress the rules that society may include in its criminal code.

A Christian perspective also includes the notion of "structural" or "communal sin". All are part of an unequal and unjust society, part of which includes the criminal justice system. And everyone falls short in terms of the "law of love" that Jesus proclaimed.

The teaching that all are involved in guilt and sin is an attempt to express a belief about the basic human condition. Even if all the other points did not apply, the truth about not being innocent would still apply, according to the Christian understanding. It is that understanding, and not any sense of respectability or moral superiority, or good fortune, that should influence the way that society should deal with those whose offending just happens to be against the criminal law.

The Centrality of Forgiveness

What wrong-doing does, in the Christian understanding, is to create a broken relationship. The brokenness may be between individuals, between an individual and society, or between individuals and God.

The brokenness between individuals and God is restored by God's reconciling love, if those individuals are prepared to accept it. His incarnation and crucifixion, his accepting the role of offender are an expression of that reconciling love, and are in pursuit of reconciliation in both social and even cosmic senses. He forgives our wrong doing, and pays the penalty for us.

> "*Forgiveness is central to the Christian Gospel.* In essence its meaning is that God forgives and accepts the offender (sinner) unconditionally if he or she trusts (has faith) in him. Good conduct (works) follows from this and does not precede it. It does not have to be earned, indeed it cannot be. Forgiveness has to be received and responded to joyfully. The gospel goes on to say that if

this is how God treats us, then this is how we must treat one another." (Preston, *The Justice Model and Forgiveness*, 1990, p. 51)

The author goes on to illustrate how forgiveness can fit in with some aspects of both the rehabilitative ideal and the justice model as understood in secular terms. He points out that forgiveness does not excuse or condone, and has to follow proper conviction for an offence. Equally it looks to change of character, as with the rehabilitative ideal, though not by forcing change on the person through punishment or therapy.

Yet forgiveness is offered with no strings attached. In the New Testament, there are no limits to, and no conditions put on God's reconciling love. You don't have to have kept the law; you don't have to belong to a particular group, tribe, nation, sect or religion; you don't have any rights to reconciliation; you can't earn it, whether by respectability, or by obedience to statute, or by good works, or by anything else. The reconciliation that God effects is described both as a gift, and as something he does as a judicial act. It is further evidence of the sort of judge God is.

This book has stressed the need to hold together biblical and theological insights with the experience of practice and with the insights of disciplines such as criminology and penology. In the New Testament there is no divide between theory and practice. Over and over again the emphasis is that if you know and believe in forgiveness then it is incumbent on you to act in the light of that — to be forgiving. The emphasis pervades both the Gospels and other writings in the New Testament:

— "Be kind to one another, tenderhearted, forgiving one another, as God has forgiven you" (Ephesians 4:32);
— "If you forgive men their trespasses, your Heavenly Father will also forgive you" (Matthew 6:14);
— "And whenever you stand praying, forgive, if you have anything against anyone, so that God may forgive you" (Mark 11:25);
— Judge not and you will not be judged, condemn not and you will not be condemned, forgive and you will be forgiven" (Luke 6:37).

Being forgiven requires personal sacrifice: it is hard. *It requires humility and a recognition of common humanity.* Could it be that both in being forgiven and in forgiving we are being essentially human?

— "So you should rather turn to forgive and comfort him, or he may be overwhelmed by excessive sorrow. So I beg you to reaffirm your love for him" (II Corinthians, 2:7);
— "If your brother sins, rebuke him, and if he repents, forgive him" (Luke, 17:3);
— "Therefore, I tell you, her sins which are many are forgiven, for she loved much; but he who is forgiven little, loves little" (Luke 7:47);
— "Father, forgive them, for they know not what they do" (Luke 23:24).

The doctrine of forgiveness caused hostile reaction then, much as the idea may occasion incredulity now as an ideal for human criminal justice. The idea of forgiveness caused particular offence to the religious hierarchy of Jesus' day. Nonetheless it is central to the New Testament's proclamation of Jesus as the Christ.

— "That you may know that the Son of Man has authority on earth to forgive sins" (Matthew 9:6);
— "Your sins are forgiven" (Mark 2:7 and Luke 5:21);
— "Who is this who even forgives sins?" (Luke 7:49);
— "In him we have redemption through his blood, the forgiveness of our trespasses" (Ephesians 1:7);
— "Through this man forgiveness is proclaimed to you" (Acts 13:38);
— "God exalted him at his right hand as Leader and Saviour to give repentance to Israel and forgiveness of sins" (Acts 5:31);
— "Anyone whom you forgive, I also forgive" (II Corinthians 2:10).

Forgiveness Leading to Reconciliation

Reconciliation is an initiative taken by God. Only as a consequence of this initiative is there the restoration of fellowship with him, and the restoration into community. This new kind of relationship is described by the New Testament as being "in Christ". A key text might be, "God was in Christ, reconciling the world to himself" (II Corinthians, 5:19). This goes beyond thinking in forensic terms, about guilt, and how to deal with it: rather it is expressed in the language of salvation and grace. The new relationship is based on grace and on God's forgiveness.

The experience of being reconciled is absolutely central in the Christian faith. The experience is one of being re-united with God from whom we have become separated as a result of our wrong-doing and imperfection. It is an experience of being accepted. There are three dimensions to, or aspects of, reconciliation.

First, experiencing reconciliation with God, one becomes reconciled with oneself, realising that you are loved by God, warts and all. Second, that in turn frees you to love your neighbour "as oneself": you can only do that if you do indeed love yourself. Third, reconciliation also extends to the community, as the reconciled person experiences acceptance by others who, like him or herself, have been touched by God's reconciling love.

The first sign of being thus touched may be a sense of penitence. This reaction can be seen as an indication that God's love is starting to have an effect.

> "Repentance, as a response to my own wrong-doing, looks back (with pain) to that wrong-doing, and forward (with hope or determination) to my own self-reform, and to the restoration of those relationships which my wrong-doing has damaged or threatened" (Duff, *Punishment, Repentance and Forgiveness*, 1990, p. 42, *et seq*).

The author suggests that this idea can serve discussions of the role of punishment in criminal justice. He goes on:

> "the ideal and proper aim of criminal punishment is to induce repentance in the unrepentant, and to provide a penitential vehicle through which that repentance can be reinforced, and appropriately expressed to others".

Here is the beginning of an idea of punishment which combines both the backward looking aspects of some theories of justice, and the forward looking ones more typically associated with the rehabilitative ideal. His ideas emphasise the relational aspect of this "communicative" idea of punishment — it involves both offender and community in dialogue and a process of rebuilding. But the notion of repentance is added into current discussions of punishment.

The Gospel proclaims the unconditional forgiveness of God and looks to reconciliation between people and the extension of forgiveness to human and social affairs. However, the institutional church has had to develop ways, some of which are conditional, for working through offences until forgiveness can be offered. Through the ages, the church has endeavoured to identify the various components of the profound transformation which takes place in this reconciling encounter between God and humanity:

— *Attrition* is sorrow concerning sin which is not necessarily intrinsic, but is rather caused by factors such as fear of punishment;

— *Contrition* is literally a "wearing away of something hard", and refers not only to outward displays of being sorry, but also to the inner experience of true heartfelt remorse. It is said to proceed not from the fear of punishment, but from the love of God;

— *Confession* is the admission of guilt, to oneself, to God and to others;

— *Supplication* is asking God to forgive the sins that have been confessed;

— *Repentance* covers both contrition and confession, but also includes the intention of making amends; it is not a condition for reconciliation, but a consequence of being touched by God's reconciling love;

— *Pardon* is pronounced by God's representative (such as a priest), after repentance and confession. It features as a regular part of Christian worship.

Society may be even less able to live by the Gospel ethic, but that ethic and offer is a standing challenge to the the practice both of society and of the church.

Theology again seems to disturb our ordinary human ideas and approaches. It is hard to see ourselves as in the same condition as some criminal: we prefer our legalism and respectability. Even our best liberalism may fall short of God's standard. There is the story of Peter asking how many times he should forgive an offending brother (Matthew 18: 21–22). He suggests seven, thinking himself generous. Jesus tells him, in effect, to forgive time without number — seventy times seven.

He goes on to tell the story of the unforgiving servant (Matthew 18:23, *et seq*). The two main points of this story are that, first, when the servant asks for mercy, the whole crippling burden of debt is written off "at a stroke"; and, second, that those who have been forgiven much should forgive others much. God's forgiveness is not conditional on our forgiving our neighbours: *but being forgiven releases in us the ability to forgive.*

This kind of thinking goes against our human and pragmatic approach. The notion of forgiving the guilty and declaring them innocent seems to be a contradiction in terms from a human standpoint. The purpose of the forgiveness, in biblical terms, is for the final restoration of the unity of all things in God their creator. It thus has a frame of reference beyond the ordering of social affairs in this life.

One reason that we may initially find the idea of forgiveness hard to take, or impractical, is that we think of it as "letting someone off". It is as if someone can offend with impunity. In the next section we shall see that forgiveness is not just a one-off response to a misdeed. Its true nature leads to newer and different kinds of behaviour. It is not that God takes offending lightly — given his nature and character as holy, he is more hurt by wrong-doing than can be appreciated in human understanding. In spite of that, forgiveness is his response to offending. But it is forgiveness within the purpose of reconciliation, and an understanding of reconciliation that leads on from the offence into new directions.

Reconciliation as Re-integration into Community

Reconciliation is both freedom from and freedom for. While the restored relationship is a gift, it brings with it obligations of responsibility on those who receive it. The sinner, being freed from his sinful past, is set free for a future of serving God. As one who is reconciled, the believer becomes an instrument of reconciliation in the world. He or she can become a messenger of reconciliation in an un-reconciled world.

In experiencing God's forgiveness, we learn what his justice is like and of his mercy. There is a fellowship or community of forgiveness, into which forgiven offenders are welcomed and accepted. This fellowship is not based on having paid a penalty, or on having achieved anything for oneself, but on the grace of God alone, and on having been forgiven. It is fellowship with God himself and with one another.

This fellowship of those who have been forgiven can proclaim, demonstrate, and mediate the forgiveness of God. Just as the experience of being loved, whether in human or religious terms, enables us to love, so the experience of being forgiven by God enables us to embark on a ministry of forgiveness. This fellowship or community of which we speak is the church.

In proclaiming, demonstrating, and mediating God's forgiveness, it does not undermine the reality of law or the nature of divine justice, but rather bears witness to their real character.

A near parallel model in the secular sphere is an agency like Alcoholics Anonymous. Alcoholics are supported by accepting they cannot solve their problems on their own. They accept the need for a power "greater than themselves", however each member may interpret that power. In fellowship with others who acknowledge that they are in the same situation and predicament, they can find strength and support to get better. It is also an important part of the treatment of alcoholics under this method that they have opportunities to help others.

There are very few "re-acceptance" procedures in our criminal justice system. The story is told of a man whose neighbour was sent to prison: on hearing that his neighbour would be released back to his home, the man expressed in disgust, "I'll have to move". Both were members of the same church!

It can be true to say that a person's real punishment begins when they are released from prison, however much they may have "paid their debt" or "tholed their assize". We are short on symbols of forgiveness and welcoming back. Our system appears to offer very little in the way of after-care — one description of after-care being that it is an "apology for vengeance", and not a very generous one.

The experience of being forgiven and being reconciled establishes a new basis for community, in the Christian understanding. It is a community of people who have received mercy and are therefore merciful. That experience of mercy incorporates a full recognition of how God judges wrong-doing. Forgiveness is no light "let-off" — it cannot be, given God's holy nature and his reaction to sin. But in this community, old hostilities and suspicions are overcome, and barriers broken down. In biblical language, Jew and Gentile, male and female, slave and free — all alike have access to God's grace (Ephesians 2:14). It does not stretch the meaning of the text if we substitute here modern pairs of opposites — for example, black and white, straight and gay, rich and poor, criminals and respectable citizens.

In another biblical picture, "he has broken down the dividing wall of partition between them" (Ephesians 2) — rather like the Berlin Wall can come down. Accepted by God, they are enabled to accept one another, and to serve the community. Perhaps community service should arise voluntarily as a result of forgiveness?!

Working through Reconciliation

Reconciliation is a process, not a one-off event, as understood in theology. It starts with God's initiative; involves an experience of forgiveness on the part of guilty people; and leads from that into a life of service and of belonging to a new community of those who have also been forgiven. To use a jargon phrase from social work and psychiatry, it is something that has to be "worked through".

Whilst this is an ongoing process in the life and experience of individuals, the Bible points to a cosmic sense in which reconciliation is in process as well. In this sense, it is a process moving towards fulfilment at the end of time.

Two things have to be said in one breath, as it were. Reconciliation has been done or "worked" in the death and resurrection of Christ. But it is also not completed, or "worked through", in that it is also the *"telos"* or ultimate aim and end of creation. Creation is still groaning under the strains of uncompleted reconciliation.

The importance of this more cosmic perspective to our present discussion is that it implies the provisionality of all efforts to translate the spirit of reconciliation into the reality of everyday life. Provisional means both temporary *and* also oriented towards the future. We can speak the word now, but the final word will be spoken at the end of time.

Our ways of dealing with offences and broken relationships can only ever hope to be a response to, and provisional reflections of, God's full reconciling love. Whilst we never see the fullness of that in this life, we undertake our activity in this connection always with an eye to that ultimate end in view.

Part 3

ACTION

Introduction

Part one began with "crime" and "punishment" as an apparently natural association of ideas. The criminal justice system was expected, by punishing crime, to achieve various objectives, such as deterrence, prevention, treatment; or to express certain responses on society's behalf, such as denunciation, retribution, just deserts. The reality, however, was much more disheartening.

Experience suggested:

— that the criminal justice system won't solve the "problem of crime";
— that it doesn't achieve the aims of deterrence, prevention, or reform;
— that expecting it to remedy social problems is a false hope;
— that a high proportion of people who come into it are already damaged;
— that it may damage many of those whose lives become caught up in its net.

Reflection on this experience produced an alternative association of ideas, namely "offence" and "reconciliation". This notion challenged, overturned and upset common ways of thinking about crime and punishment. It questioned ordinary assumptions about innocence and guilt. It emphasised a common human predicament, and a communal rather than an individual responsibility for crime and for the wrong-doer.

This section of the book attempts to suggest to what values the criminal justice system might give expression, and what aims it might have, in the light of reflection based on Christian belief and theology. It does not attempt to give a blueprint for what a Christian criminal justice system might look like, but it does suggest what values and aims would receive endorsement from a Christian perspective. If these aims and values commend themselves, others will need to work out their detailed application to the life and workings of the system as it currently operates.

This third section will itself be comprised of three parts. There will be a movement of focus from the general to the particular. First, fundamental values and aims which might characterise a criminal justice system are suggested. Then a number of illustrations and examples are given of selected schemes or ventures in which some elements of these ideas are contained or expressed. Finally a number of practical suggestions for action are put forward as a starting place for change.

Basic Values and Affirmations

The "crisis" in the criminal justice system, which figures in the title, is about *values and aims*. There is a vacuum that some want to fill with the idea of punishment. We want to resist that move for a number of reasons, one of them being that the idea of punishment can so easily become a cloak that makes punitiveness respectable or legitimate. Theology offers alternative values and ideals.

Christian belief suggests that a *number of different values* should characterise the workings of the criminal justice system, and the way it should respond to people who offend.

Here are ten values that could be described as "first order" principles for criminal justice. Each has a negative correlate, which is often found in the criminal justice system as it currently operates. We met these negative aspects in our experience, described in part one. Part two suggests the alternative values derived from theology. We express that set of values as ten "affirmations", showing, for each value, the negative aspect we wish to shun.

1 We affirm *love and goodness* as basic values for humanity, and therefore reject a response to people who offend which seeks to repay evil with evil;

2 We affirm an understanding of *justice as rooted in mercy*, and therefore reject vengeance as an unacceptable response to offending;
3 We affirm *forgiveness as the preferred response* to broken relationships, and reject punitiveness as corrosive of a humane society;
4 We affirm *reconciliation as the ultimate aim in responding to offending*, and therefore ostracism and rejection of offenders are to be avoided;
5 We affirm *the value of mutual responsibility* between members of society, and reject any denial of that responsibility by way of scapegoating;
6 We affirm *the basic human dignity and worth of every individual*, and therefore reject any degrading treatment of people who offend;
7 We affirm that *every human being has the potential for growth*, and therefore reject any denial of opportunity, and imposition of humiliation;
8 We affirm *the need of every human being both to give and to receive*, and reject any exclusion of offenders through suppression and silencing;
9 We affirm *the creation of relationships as an essential part* of being human, and reject any exclusion of offenders from this process;
10 We affirm *the community dimension of all human life*, and therefore reject any neglect or dehumanisation of people who offend by the larger community.

Expressed like this, and at this level of generality, it might be hard to disagree with the suggested list of positive values given. It is easy to assent to ideals, and it may seem of little practical use to spend time on them.

It is important to have ideals and aspirations. It is important to have goals towards which we strive, and against which actual achievements can be measured. Without them the system is in danger of becoming mechanical, inhuman and brutal, and society too suffers. People working in the system need support and motivation. Part of the reason for the crisis in criminal justice is that one ideal, that of rehabilitation, is regarded as suspect. The failure of the "treatment" model to "work" (like the failure of other objectives such as deterrence to "work") allows for a debate about morals and values, rather than mere techniques. It is crucial to have some values other than punitiveness operative in the criminal justice system. It is as important to ask about the nature of the system and the values it embodies, as to question its practical results.

Any "evaluation" of the system has to ask questions about values. If the answer is given solely in terms of "value for money" that is itself a statement about values. It is a moral judgment about the place of money as the arbiter of all things.

In an imperfect world, there may have to be control, some degree of confinement, and less than perfect systems and régimes. These should not be the first line or even normal responses to offending. When they have to be used, there could be a sense of sadness about the failure that recourse to them inevitably signifies. Each time second best is all that can be achieved, there should be an examination of how else the situation might have been managed.

To many people values and ideals of this kind seem "soft". They appear not to take crime seriously. *Understood from a Christian perspective, this is a mis-interpretation.* Christian belief emphasises the character of God as perfect in goodness, holiness, righteousness and love. It is precisely because of this experience of God that Christians react with extreme seriousness and horror to the hurt and harm and violence that criminal conduct sometimes involves, and to the evil that this represents.

Christian belief *goes on from there* to point to the suffering and pain undergone by Jesus at the hands of humanity — especially that inflicted by "respectable" authority, both secular and religious. Forgiveness is much the most "painful" and "costly" option all round — costly in terms that simple economics cannot comprehend. If "hard" responses to crime are desired, then Christian faith points to the hardest of all. But it is not the easy-to-achieve get-tough policies which it points towards, but rather the profoundly difficult work of understanding and responding humanely to the tragedy of crime.

Even if one assents to ideals like these, there is no guarantee that they will necessarily find expression in the criminal justice system. It is easy to pay lip service to them in theory, but then not to operate them in practice. "The good I would I do not," complained St Paul, in an accurate reflection on the human condition (Romans 7:16). But at the moment there is little recognition in society of the "good" to be adopted and pursued.

Stated simply as a list, the ideals may seem abstract, and unlikely to inspire action. The values should be seen as objectives to pursue, concepts and instructions to obey and to be guided by. The theological reflection also emphasised the idea of the ultimate or "*telos*" towards which to work. To borrow, and indeed *rework*, a vogue word of today, they are the "targets" we should aim to achieve.

Objectives of Criminal Justice

Do Justice and Love Mercy

If the list above represents the kind of values that Christian belief suggests should characterise the criminal justice system, then the injunction "do justice and love mercy" might serve as a title for the objectives of criminal justice (Micah 6:8). The linking of ideas — justice and mercy — is important. The emergent "justice model" has important criticisms of the excesses of "welfare-ism". But it also has important limitations: the danger of it reducing matters to mere legalism ("due process" notions), or of it giving renewed emphasis to the "just deserts" philosophy. On both these counts it is found wanting from the perspective of Christianity.

Hopes that the system can "solve the problem of crime" may need to be abandoned. In particular the idea that the infliction of punishment by a criminal justice system will significantly deter offenders or prevent the commission of crime by others has been shown to be unsupported. Crime is a multi-faceted phenomenon; it has many causes. To think that a single focus response from a monolithic system will constitute the "answer" to it is fallacious.

It is precisely because society's initial expectation is that the system should "stop crime" that the point needs to be underlined further. Recent years have seen an increased emphasis on "law and order" as the seemingly natural response to behaviour of any kind that troubles society, or its dominant sections. A lot of money has flowed from this emphasis: into increasing levels of pay and staffing in police and prison services, in embarking on massive programmes of prison building, and in paying for the very lengthy sentences now routinely given for some kinds of crime. That money has therefore not been available for other purposes which, arguably, might have been more "valuable". The emphasis on "law and order", and the way it is interpreted, have been described as "often approaching the quality of a secular religion" (Morris, *Consensus versus Ideology — Problems for Contemporary Penal Policy*, 1990, p. 60).

> "All penal questions are political questions, in that they concern not merely the issues of *criminal* justice in its narrowest sense, but *social* justice in a broader context. Overwhelmingly those who appear before the courts are drawn disproportionately from the ranks of the poor, the disadvantaged or the socially marginal," continues the author.

How the criminal justice sytem deals with people at present tends towards the exacerbation of disadvantage and marginality. It may exacerbate injustice rather than rectify it.

Religion has been expected to support the dominant view of law and order. Where people have called attention to the social dimensions of justice, and stressing responsibilities for crime which go beyond the individual, they have been criticised as offering "sociological alibis" for criminals. However, the New Testament contains a number of telling stories in which "respectable" people offer excuses for not attending to issues that are right under their noses (those who "passed by on the other side" in the story of the Good Samaritan) (Luke 10:33, *et seq*); or who have other preoccupations (attending to property, getting married) when invited to come into God's Kingdom of justice and righteousness (Luke 14:15, *et seq*).

In total contrast to any view that Christianity should necessarily uncritically support any particular current view of "law and order", we suggest that *there are three important objectives to pursue:*

1 to keep some kinds or categories of people out of the criminal justice system altogether;
2 to explore ways of responding to socially unacceptable behaviour which do not involve the use of the criminal justice system at all;
3 to respond justly to those people who need to be dealt with by the criminal justice system — the important emphasis being to respond justly to the people, not punitively to the crime.

Diversion

The criminal justice system is a negative system; it tends to damage and disadvantage. It is not, on the whole, a system for doing good. Some matters should be dealt with without recourse to the system at all.

1 *No one under the age of 18 should come into the criminal justice system:*
Scotland has led the way in dealing with children and young people who get into trouble — including committing what in an adult would be responded to as crimes — without recourse to a court or punishment based system (see, for example, Moore, *Guide to the Children's Hearings*, 1989). The Children's Hearing System currently deals with young people up to the age of 16, and thus already covers an age range which can be quite a prolific one in terms of committing crime. The Hearing seeks to engage young people and families in "round table" discussion of what may lie behind the trouble, and tries to find measures of care to resolve the situation.

The point is not that a care system may be better or worse than a punishment system in terms of preventing or deterring offending. What is claimed is that this way of handling the problem is less damaging for all concerned, and is more likely to avoid locking young people into the stigma and career of crime. The idea is that the system seeks to respond to wrong-doing in young people along a different path altogether, and with different objectives. There is no pretence that wrong-doing is not intrinsically serious, or that it will not be responded to. But Scotland has opted to respond to young people in need and trouble by having a system whose prime objective is not to punish them, or to focus solely on the wrong they have done, but instead to deal constructively and creatively with the situation insofar as this is possible.

We propose that the system should now be extended to include young people up to the age of 18. There may need to be arrangements, as there already are for under 16s, whereby some extremely serious matters are dealt with by a court, and there will need to be new kinds of resources to deal with the different needs of this age group. But the important point is to move away from a punishment approach as being the normal, first line response to every misdemeanour committed by these young people.

2 *The principle of diversion should be extended to adults*:
There are many examples and instances of adults needlessly being dealt with by the process of prosecution, court, and punishment. They may have various needs, problems, incapacities, and conditions, which bear on their offending and degree of culpability; which are not addressed by the business of punishment; and which may be exacerbated as a result of the way the system deals with people. This does not seem just, and is certainly not very humane.

The system should not be expected to provide the answers to those needs, problems, and so on, but it should take account of them in assessing responsibility, and determining how to respond to wrong-doing. Resources to help people in these circumstances should be available as a part of the community's ordinary arrangements, and people should not be penalised at the hands of the criminal justice system for want of those resources being available. Equally people should not be able to evade the consequences of deeds for which they can reasonably and rightly be held responsible. They should also not be assisted to evade facing up to the people whose lives may have been harmed by their behaviour, even if they could be regarded as not being entirely responsible for their behaviour.

In a number of parts of Scotland in recent years, Procurators Fiscal have initiated schemes, in conjunction with social work departments and voluntary agencies, to explore the possibilities of some people in need being referred for help and assistance, rather than being prosecuted. There is a potentially interesting shift in habits of thought from finding reasons not to prosecute (and regarding this as exceptional) to the more funda-mental question of what are the grounds on which something as rigorous and significant as a prosecution, with all that it entails, is justified.

As a rule, these schemes are based on looking at cases on an individual basis, and assessing — often from limited information given in police reports of the crime — whether some background factor is hinted at which may bear on the matter and be worthy of exploration.

We would like to *see a more systematic exploration of this idea*, and suggest some general categories of situa-tion, or instances, where there might be a *predisposition to avoid* prosecution, rather than the reverse.

a) There might be a prejudice in cases involving elderly people in favour of using diversion if at all possible. This is not to imply that all elderly people should be regarded as not being responsible for their actions, and should thus escape the possibility of prosecution. But it is to say that the factor of age should trigger a response which automatically explores whether factors associated with age, such as infirmity, declining mental and social skills, confusion and frailty, might not be factors influencing the offence. And it is to say that, even if such factors do not apply, every attempt to avoid prosecution should nonetheless be considered.

b) People who are mentally ill deserve especially careful consideration. There is accumulating evidence of an alarming proportion of people being held in prison who are mentally ill. Often it appears to be the case that the penal system ends up dealing with such people because of the reluctance or incapacity of other social and health services to take such people.

c) People who commit offences under the influence of drink or drugs, might be considered along the following lines:

> At one end of the scale there are some who harm no one but themselves, and whose behaviour is clearly the outcome of a serious problem of addiction. In these instances it seems wrong that the criminal justice system should have to deal with them, and that they should have to come into its embrace. Yet they do so in considerable numbers. The obvious need is for detoxification and rehabilitative services in the community. The absence of these should not excuse the abuse which resorting to the penal system involves;
>
> At the other end there are people who, with various degrees of addiction, may do considerable harm — often whilst in charge of a motor vehicle — whilst under the immediate influence of drink or drugs. Here the system needs to ensure that two things happen: first that any need for treatment is explored and taken up if required; and second, that — subsequently to that treatment if necessary — the person does not evade the consequences of their behaviour, and is dealt with justly, as we outline below.

In many instances, there will have to be a balance of considerations — of the extent to which an addiction reduces culpability and requires treatment, as against not allowing people to avoid the consequences of their behaviour.

d) Women offenders may experience particular hardship at the hands of the criminal justice system, because at one and the same time they are perceived as being in trouble because of "problems", and yet no one wants to deal with those problems. It is an inappropriate punishment to use prison either to deal with a "problem" or because no one else will.

e) People who are homeless, who are poor, who may have histories of being abused as children, can experience extra penalties at the hands of the penal system as it currently operates. They may be denied bail, imprisoned for non-payment of fines, suffer within prison, not so much because of what they did, but because of their personal situation or a social problem. Prison should not be a backstop for inadequacies in other areas of social provision.

A rounded approach to justice requires that account be taken of factors which in varying degrees may influence or even compel offending, and which reduce in varying ways the person's level of culpability.

A humane system needs both to be in a position to refer people for any treatment that is needed and to be able to respond appropriately to the person's level of responsibility. The principle of diversion draws attention to the need to justify any prosecution as a serious, and potentially damaging experience; and it looks to explore the possibilities for problems being addressed in more constructive ways. Scotland has led the way in adopting this principle in respect of children who get into trouble, and that experience has also provided practical experience of how it can be done, and can win public support. There is now considerable potential for applying the idea in respect of many adults, and thus helping to create a more humane criminal justice system.

Reparation and Mediation
(As a Second Objective of Criminal Justice)

Every day, people in many different situations encounter conflicts and attempt to resolve them. Family members, neighbours, friends, or respected local figures may step in to help two parties to reach an agreement. And every day there are examples of people attempting to repair a relationship by offering an apology, a gift, or a service. In a more formalised way, and on a larger scale, we are familiar with mediation in the industrial field: for example, with ACAS assisting conflicting parties to reach an agreement. Many matters could better be thought of as conflicts that could be resolved by mediation and/or various forms of reparation. The absence of ways of resolving situations through mediation may result in the calling of the Police and the definition of the situation as a crime.

The workings of the criminal justice system often leave the victim out in the cold. The system deals with offenders in non-relational ways — simply taking money away from them, and not dealing with whatever may have been behind the offending, whether personal problem, or relationship breakdown. The infliction of punishment often leads to a sense of embitterment and alienation rather than creating a sense of personal or social responsibility.

Mediation and reparation schemes are increasingly being tried as an alternative way of responding to many situations that are initially reported as crimes. It is being claimed for them that they do offer scope for the inclusion of the victim in the situation; that they do encourage offenders to face up to what they have done and become aware of the consequences of their behaviour; and that they do offer the possibility of meeting, including forms of reconciliation and even forgiveness.

Describing the first scheme of its kind in Scotland, its leading practitioner, Robert MacKay, writes: "the primary postulate is that reparation with a view to the reconciliation of the parties where possible, and of both the parties to society, are not subsidiary aims of criminal justice, but are central and integral to it" (MacKay, *Reparation in Criminal Justice*, 1988, p. 67). This scheme did involve cases which had been reported as crimes and were seen as serious enough to warrant court proceedings, but involved an attempt to mediate and arrange reparation as an alternative to court and punishment imposed by that means.

Responding Justly to Offenders
(as a Third Objective of Criminal Justice)

The criminal justice system in Scotland draws more and more people into its embrace; it uses its ultimate weapon, imprisonment, to a much greater extent than its European counterparts; and it sends a rising proportion of prisoners to long periods of imprisonment which would be unheard of elsewhere. All this is done in the name of justice. Given that the use of diversion, and of reparation and mediation, may be expanded, we suggest that, for those people who have to be dealt with by the system, the aim should be — drawing from theological understandings of justice — to "respond justly to offenders".

The phrase suggests activity, a process, pursuit of an objective — not simply an abstract value or vague ideal. Justice is not so much a disturbed equilibrium that has to be restored, as a creative opportunity to make and renew relationships. Theology suggests that justice is something that has been "worked for us" by God, but has to be "worked through" in our experience. There are various stages from penitence through to the experience of acceptance and pardon, and the emergence of a desire to serve within a forgiven community. That is the kind of "due process" to aim for.

Using that kind of paradigm, the crucial elements in the process of responding justly to offenders, drawing from a theological approach, should be:

1 *Asserting that the behaviour was wrong*:
   Theology and Christian belief take offending, evil, sin very seriously. But they seek to do so without condemnation of the whole person. One item of wrong or evil behaviour is not seen as constituting irrevocable evidence that the person is totally depraved.

   Christian belief points as well to the basic human condition of fallenness. There is no ground for any sense of moral superiority; none of us is entitled to throw the first stone. Theology emphasises the community's share in responsibility for injustice; its close involvement with offenders in their offending; and its working together with the offender to overcome that wrong-doing.

The phrase "asserting that the behaviour was wrong" is deliberately chosen in place of more familiar words from the criminal justice context such as "denunciation" and "condemnation". The phrase is emphatic and energetic but seeks to avoid the worst aspects of righteous indignation, which is out of place. It suggests more of a levelling as between judge and offender than the imposition and expression of social displeasure from above.

2 *Exploring the person's awareness of the wrong-doing*: Again the choice of words seeks to avoid possible dangers in current terminology about "confronting the person with their offence".

The idea of "consciousness raising" may be another way of describing this objective. Many offenders may not feel that what they did was wrong, or may seek to justify it by reference to personal circumstances such as disadvantage, inequality, alienation, and so on. The exploration of their awareness of their wrong-doing, and any attempts to raise their consciousness of it, will reveal something about their relationship with the wider society, and maybe about wider social injustices in that society.

The idea of "doing justice" looks to the improvement and enhancing of that relationship. Consciousness raising is not a one sided matter in this context; it is a relational one. Awareness of offence is a necessary prelude to meaningful forgiveness and restoration.

3 *Assisting the person with the consequences of his or her offending*:
Help and assistance, properly understood, should be essential characteristics of a criminal justice system. The activity of advising, assisting, and befriending, should not be confined to the supervision of probationers, but should be central aspects of the whole system's working.

The phrase "assisting the person with the consequences of his or her offending" deliberately includes assistance to the person, including assistance with whatever personal and social difficulties he or she may have as an individual — *and* in relation to the consequences of his or her offending. This second part of the phrase is deliberately chosen too. The current vogue for punishment has found expression in social workers and probation officers becoming more "offence focussed", to the reduction in importance of their helping role. Both have to be kept in "focus".

The phrase incorporates the consequences of offending both for the person themselves *and* for others.

The concept of help suggested by the theological paradigm can include:

— assistance with the person's feelings of remorse;
— the possibilities of reparation and reconciliation;
— giving service to the community;
— working through to new patterns of behaviour and relationships.

Here indeed is a radical and wide ranging concept of help that should appeal to the distinctive social work philosophy of the Scottish Social Work Departments. It might provide that sense of mission and idealism that is needed to inspire the new organisational arrangements. The concept should go well beyond mere "social work" and should imbue the whole workings of the system, whether in court, in the community, or in prison.

4 *Looking to the re-integration of the person into the community:*
"Society," wrote Oscar Wilde, "takes upon itself the right to inflict appalling punishment on the individual, but when the man's punishment is over, it leaves him to himself. It abandons him at the moment when its highest duty towards him begins" (quoted in Fox, *The English Prison and Borstal System*, 1952). There is within the current criminal justice system a very limited concept of "after-care", but its place and priority, never very great, have been downgraded in recent years.

The objective of re-integration is again not to be thought of solely in relation to imprisonment, but as a central objective of the whole system's workings. There are many rituals for condemnation and exclusion, but very few for re-acceptance and re-integration. In Christian worship and practice the pronouncement of pardon or absolution is a regular feature. We need to explore ways in which like rituals can become a part of practice in criminal justice.

E

5   *Asking whether others need to be protected from the person*:
There are some circumstances in which deprivation of
liberty is justified. Deprivation of liberty is a gross thing,
and the extent to which it is currently used suggests a
degree of desensitisation as to the enormity of what is
involved. Many of the existing justifications — deterrence,
reformation, denunciation — now appear inadequate.

The grounds for the just deprivation of liberty will not
have to do so much with the infliction of punishment, as
with the protection of others or society in general from
people who are intent on inflicting very serious harm on
those others or that society. There is much argument over
the application of the term "dangerousness": many
people currently deemed dangerous are not, while others
— such as corporations which disregard health and safety
laws, drunken drivers — are.

The reality that such danger exists from some people's
behaviour and psychological state is not denied by
Christian belief. It accepts the existence of evil and hopes
to be able to recognise it — in all its various forms. But it
looks still to overcome that evil with good.

Justice in this circumstance will also require that
conditions in custody will seek to avoid those negative
values listed at the start of this section. The process — to
be aimed for in custody as much as in any other part of the
criminal justice system — will still have to do with
exploring the person's awareness of their offending,
helping them deal with its consequences, and looking to
their reintegration into the community.

6   *Objectives of doing justice — a Summary*:
Theology suggests that the prime aim of doing justice
should not be the infliction of punishment/pain. Rather
the aim is at all times to be on the look-out for:

— opportunities to repair and restore broken relationships;
— ways of making new relationships where they are non-
   existent;
— finding other ways of resolving disputes and conflicts;
— considering whether any offence is an outcome of
   social injustice;
— giving help to all affected by offending;

— looking to reintegrate wrong-doers back into community;
— finding ways for the community to be involved in the system;
— looking to find a way forward rather than simply restoring a status-quo.

We have suggested ten values that the system should seek to express and have as ideals. We have suggested three broad aims for the system. We argued that there are some aims the system should abandon. We sketched in new habits of thought that need to be acquired. We summarised the system's aim as being "to respond justly to offenders" — provided always the aims of keeping out, and trying to sort things out have been tried first.

The heading "do justice and love mercy" is an injunction from the prophet Micah in the Old Testament (Micah 6:8). What neither the Old Testament, or even a criminal justice system, can entirely legislate for is the law of love as exemplified in Jesus, or the kind of "justice" that involves him as an innocent person who takes our offences, both individual and collective, on himself. That law and that example remain our inspiration and ultimate ideal, something we seek to attain to, but which goes beyond law and justice as understood in human terms.

Looking to the End of Punishment

Introduction

Theology often overturns familiar ways of thinking. Can it turn the backward looking approach of punishment around? Theology has a frame of reference which also looks to the end of things, especially in the sense of their goal. It looks to the end of punishment, in two senses — its cessation, and its objective.

This section comprises some examples and illustrations of ways of responding to offenders that already express some of the ideas and approaches which we have been proposing. They suggest that these approaches can be effective. They are not meant as a comprehensive survey, or necessarily as an advertisement for particular schemes. Nor are they hard evidence that particular schemes work or generally produce the kinds of results described here. But they do identify starting points and instructive examples which are worth pursuing and building upon.

The illustrations will be grouped under three broad headings. These will be — reparation; giving service and restoring relationships; and offering opportunities. We will seek to give examples from different stages of the criminal justice process — encompassing pre-court situations, non-custodial measures, and instances drawn from penal institutions.

Reparation

Example One

During an outburst of crowd misbehaviour, damage was done to the car of a woman who was eight months pregnant at the time, and who had no relationship at all to the crowd or any kind of involvement in the disturbance. A young man was arrested for the damage. If he had gone to court he would have acquired a record, and possibly been fined. He would not have met the victim or had to think much about the offence, other than in terms of paying over money to an impersonal office at the court.

Instead the Procurator Fiscal reading the Police Report of this incident referred the matter to a Reparation and Mediation Scheme. This involved a Mediator approaching the young man and asking if he was prepared for an approach in turn to be made to the victim to see if she was prepared to accept some form of reparation from him.

The young man agreed to the approach being made. It transpired that the woman wanted to achieve two things. She wanted compensation for the damage to the car, but in particular she wanted the young man to appreciate her feelings of terror and anxiety, especially in view of her pregnancy. The young man agreed to pay the money, and she accepted the reality that he could only do so by instalments; he also, much more "painfully", agreed to meet her and listen to her experiences and concerns. The agreement arranged by the Mediator was kept by the young man, and as a result the Fiscal decided not to take the case to court.

This is one example taken from a description by Robert MacKay of a pre-court reparation and mediation scheme. MacKay's study and experience led him to conclude that, "the chief benefits that can be achieved by reparation agreements, and by no other means so well, are:

— the ending of feuds or their prevention;
— the negotiation of financial or material amends;
— the possibility of improving or restoring relationships;
— the chance for the victim to face the offender personally with the consequences of the offence;
— the pre-emption of retaliation" (MacKay, *Reparation in Criminal Justice*, 1988, p. 38).

Example Two

In an English scheme, reparation was attempted at a stage when a case had come to court, but before sentence. The Court still had to impose a sentence even after the mediation had been tried. This scheme particularly sought to emphasise meetings between offender and victim. "One young man agreed to meet a couple he had burgled. After a nervous start, they answered a lot of each others questions about the offence, and then moved into an exchange of mutual advice. At the end of the meeting they rode away on the bus together. The young man thought it had changed his life, and he has not been in trouble since." The experience of meeting the victim was seen by the offender as being a tough option.

Example Three

Another example of a scheme that seeks to improve understanding and dialogue between offenders and victims is based at a Youth Custody Centre. Here a group comprising equal numbers of offenders and victims meet over a number of weeks. The victims who participate are not those directly injured by the offenders with whom they discuss their experiences — rather the aim is to have people who have committed, or been victim of, similar kinds of offences.

Mediation and meeting can also have unanticipated consequences for victims. The victim may find that he or she recognises in the offender not a faceless monster, but a fellow human being. This "demythologising" of the offender may in turn serve to reduce the victim's sense of insecurity, fear, and isolation.

These examples and schemes show the possibilities that mediation and arranging meetings offer for creating an opportunity for making amends, and even for new attitudes — on the part of victim, offender, and personnel within the criminal justice system. Part one described the present system, and its punishment based emphasis, as non-relational. Whilst existing laws do allow some scope for financial compensation, they do not as yet ensure any meeting, any prospect for repairing a broken relationship.

There is little doubt of the affinity between aspects of mediation and reparation, as they are emerging in these examples and schemes, and the biblical notion of reconciliation. There is the painful process of facing up to past wrong. There is the vulnerability of offering forgiveness and the humility of accepting it. There is a commitment to a new, reconstituted relationship, which does not ignore, or even simply return to, the past, but incorporates the breach within the new relationship as a healed wound.

Giving Service and Restoring Relationships

Example One

In 1969 a group of Borstal boys attended a camp at Aultbea in Wester Ross along with a group of children in need of special care from the Camphill Rudolf Steiner School in Aberdeen. This led to the formation of an organisation called the Six Circle Group, which in the intervening years has run 49 camps, involving 2,300 people from 80 agencies working with the physically and mentally handicapped, the socially disadvantaged, and offenders from Young Offenders' Institutions, Cornton Vale women's prison, and some 30 people serving life sentences. The Six Circle Group is now contemplating moving into a full time day centre project in a designated urban priority area. The aim of the organisation is to promote mutual community service between those generally seen as receivers rather than givers of service, and is expressed in the motto, "in meeting the needs of others you meet the needs in yourself".

Example Two

Community service is a popular disposal with the courts, and seems also to appeal to a wider public. Seen merely as a "punishment", community service can be a way of shaming people and making them do menial work — a sort of latter-day equivalent of the chain gang. The government's new guidelines want to build in this "hard physical work" emphasis.

Thankfully many of those who run such schemes have a larger vision, and have found opportunities for people to do unpaid work that brings them into contact with others, often people in some sort of need. Their emphasis is both on "service", and on "community" in a much more relational sense than simply "not being in prison".

One Community Service Organiser wrote "from unlikely places can emerge some very talented individuals. The experience of seeing such people shine during their time with us reassures me about the basic 'normality' of those who appear at court on criminal matters. Some arrive with obvious tailor made skills; Richard had done photography in the services and is using his knowledge to run a photography class for the voluntary leaders in a community centre, who in turn will pass it on to their youth club members" (Lothian Region Social Work Department *Newsletter*, 1987, no. 1).

Example Three

The same organiser reports a different illustration where a member of the community who knew the person in trouble took the initiative. When one of his youth club members got into trouble he arranged that the young person became his assistant leader as his community service task. He took a great risk, and offered valuable support and guidance. The growth in the young person's maturity and confidence is a tribute to the manager's faith. The young person is now thinking of staying on as assistant leader once his official sentence is finished. Here is an example of an initiative being taken by somebody who had been "offended against", as it were, to restore and rebuild the confidence of someone who had offended. The element of risk and faith involved means that sometimes such initiatives will come to grief, but it is precisely this willingness to go the extra mile which makes for humane and satisfying justice (ibid).

Example Four

The idea that the use of a relationship with someone might be a healing or restorative technique was a central notion in the "treatment model". That the particular theories may have fallen from grace does not invalidate the more fundamental point about the making and restoring of relationships. One probation officer had a larger idea of this than simply his own relationship with his probationers.

He writes: "experience of transporting kids across the country to various institutions left me with the distinct impression that city kids really did miss out on a wealth of experience. Trees and cows were a cause for comment, while mountains were a distant vision, and calculated to remain so. Taking a deep breath, I raided the court poor box to equip ten candidates, selected on the basis of high risk potential and general unacceptability with the necessary boots and clothes, and persuaded one of the Magistrates to give us the use of a cottage previously reserved for the Duke of Edinburgh's award scheme.

"I like to think that somewhere along the line they learned that great things are done when men and mountains meet, and that, the repeated lessons of making a half pint last for half an hour in the village pub while engaging the locals in conversation were at least as useful as the same amount of time spent listening to my advice in the probation office. I hope there was an effect on the 'locals' too when they discovered to whom they were talking" (Lothian Region Social Work Department *Newsletter*, 1987, no. 2).

The experience of giving service and restoring relationships can lead to a breaking down of barriers. In 1981, the International Year of the Disabled, staff and inmates of Scottish Prisons undertook various tasks, both locally and nationally, as a result of which they raised £50,000 for the deaf. Three prisons have for over 20 years provided braille services for the blind. Schemes which break down the divisions between offenders and others, and which make new, or re-make old, relationships should have widespread support.

Offering Opportunities

These examples have already shown that ideas of reparation, of giving service and restoring relationships, can be found right across the spectrum of criminal justice. They need not be confined to formal orders such as probation and community service, or to separate schemes of reparation. Examples have been found in custodial situations too.

Example One

Much of the equipment and fittings in a house which is used for people on probation was made by prisoners serving long sentences. In developing this house to provide an alternative to custody, great emphasis was placed in the publicity on the residents not being an undue risk to the courts or to the community. Yet that facility was helped to come about by the efforts of prisoners who themselves did not necessarily have the opportunity for such an alternative to being in prison at the time they were sentenced.

Example Two

A scheme in Dumbarton incorporates a mix of doing unpaid work, of receiving help, and of meeting victims. "The work is designed to make them face up to their reasons for offending and to accept responsibility for what they have done. The sessions also make offenders confront the effects of their crimes on the wider community: they include meetings with counsellors from the local victims' support group. Many have found a new purpose: Anthony, a former car thief, has realised an ambition to train as a hairdresser; Mark has trained as a volunteer so that he can work to keep other young people out of trouble. Michael, once a persistent housebreaker, sums up the feeling of many at the centre when he says, 'I feel like I've done a 180 degree turn around'" (Dumbarton Division of Strathclyde Social Work Department, 14.2.90).

"The short sharp shock has been tried and simply does not work: prison is a very ineffective way of stopping young people from offending. In many cases prison simply turns out to be a 'school for crime'. [This scheme] allows vulnerable young people the chance to be counselled and supported out of a criminal phase" (ibid).

Example Three

The Scottish Prison Service has developed schemes of "Special Escorted Leaves" for prisoners as part of a possible programme leading to release from a long sentence. The visit allowed for the prisoner to go out under escort for a specific period, and could include visits to the person's family. One aspect of these schemes was that the Prison Officer doing the escort did it in his own time, and the prisoner had to find an officer who would volunteer to do the escort. Whilst it could have the invidious effect of making prisoners dependent on the grace and favour of officers, it does show that officers do "dare to care" and give of their time.

Also a scheme of "Training for Freedom" was instituted which allowed some prisoners nearing their release date to live in a hostel apart from the main halls of the prison, though still within the walls, but to go out to work each day and be trusted to come back in the evening. As the scheme developed, and as paid employment opportunities were scarce, people on such schemes undertook various forms of community service, again in settings which involved them having to meet with and relate to others.

Example Four

In a similar vein, the Scottish Girl Guide Association allowed a Ranger Guide Service Unit to be formed of borstal girls at Cornton Vale, and the unit took its place in the County Division of Girl Guides. The borstal girls went out into the community on projects with the handicapped and sick, in hospitals, and in schools for the deaf and mentally subnormal. The work encouraged feelings of responsibility and sense of worth in the women, and made them realise that many other people were worse off than they were. They also participated in the annual camps and meetings of the Girl Guide Association.

Example Five

No book on penal issues in Scotland can be complete without a mention of the Barlinnie Special Unit.

The unit was set up in response to the problem of dealing within the ordinary prison system with "Scotland's most violent men" (Carrel, *The Special Unit, Barlinnie Prison*). The basic concept was the involvement of each prisoner, not only in his own treatment, but with that of his fellow inmates. Staff and inmates endeavoured to see themselves as a single community with mutually acceptable aims.

"It was a brave act of faith in a relatively small number of prison officers and prisoners that made the Unit a reality," wrote one observer (ibid). Another commented that one factor making for shared interest and common cause between prisoners and staff was the intensity of the risk and the awareness of the level of potential criticism from outside.

The critics had said that it couldn't be done in Scotland: there was so much aggression and violence in the Scottish character, especially in the men, and the moral climate is so different from other countries. The Unit has shown that it can be done, and there is a moral that goes well beyond the prison walls.

"It is a sign of what transformation could take place in this country if the people in all parts were given opportunity and encouragement to respect their own and each other's humanity, and to develop their personalities in creative action" (ibid). Jimmy Boyle, perhaps the Unit's most famous prisoner, entitled his first book, *A Sense of Freedom.*

Example Six

In recent times, the Scottish Prison Service has been issuing discussion documents, holding meetings, and running seminars in which prisoners are given a voice. In October 1989 a two day conference took place in Peterhead Prison and involved prisoners as well as staff, academics, and administrators, and discussed the idea of small units. The Conference had been preceded by 3 weeks of joint planning involving staff and inmates, to ensure that all could put items on the agenda. Building on the success of this initial venture, further conferences were held — at Perth in September 1990, on the subject of pre-release schemes; at Edinburgh in October 1990 on HIV/AIDS; and at Shotts in November on problems of life imprisonment. There are plans for similar conferences in 1991 on issues of drugs and of sex offenders. Recent policy statements — such as "Custody and Care" and "Opportunity and Responsibility" — are signs of a movement towards minimal standards, greater respect for inmates, and other values to which only lip service may previously have been the order of the day. In some respects ideas from the Special Unit are being adopted in the mainstream of prison life. There is a new degree of openness here which allows not only for public debate, but also for prisoners to be involved in formulating policy about their own conditions and life.

Conclusion

These illustrations and examples show that people in the system are finding ways of taking risks, arranging meetings, dealing in relationships, introducing innovations. These schemes have their problems as well, and there is not necessarily any more guarantee of "success" than there is with punishment approaches. But there is at least the guarantee of a system that will express better values and pursue better aims than those which it replaces.

Recommendations

In this final section we set out recommendations arising from our discussion to each of the three audiences we seek to address.

Recommendations to the Public

1 Get to know more about the criminal justice system and its workings. Respond to any opportunities it offers to discuss its operations.
2 Become more practically involved in its workings — become a prison visitor; become a volunteer; offer community service opportunities for offenders; offer employment openings to people in trouble.
3 Encourage both the media and your elected representatives to support humane and forward looking policies in relation to crime and criminals.
4 Support those working in the system in the pursuit of humane innovation, and in taking some risks.
5 Recognise natural feelings of vengeance and punitiveness in attitudes to criminals, but do not let these feelings dictate actions and policies.
6 Support and maybe involve yourself with a local victims support scheme.
7 Look for indications that the commission of a crime may be a pointer to social injustice, or what it may tell us about ourselves and our society.
8 Reflect on the values and objectives that might characterise our criminal justice system. Consider the ideals and values suggested by Christianity, whether or not the faith itself is one that you would necessarily accept.

Recommendations to Policy Makers and Practitioners in the System

1 Be proactive, not reactive. Develop a positive vision for the system. Come together to create that vision and share it with society at large.
2 Campaign for an integrated policy for criminal justice. Argue more strongly and more collectively for the resources for a humane system.
3 Consider ways of broadening the idea of culpability as it is currently understood and operated. Reflect on the concept of varying degrees of capacity or responsibility as being more realistic and constructive.
4 The "justice model" is an inadequate basis for policy in criminal justice. Examine the potential application of Christian concepts of justice.
5 Develop new ways — such as diversion, and mediation/reparation — to keep people from coming into the system in the first place.
6 Diversify both the extent of use, and the styles of implementation, of existing orders such as probation and community service. Be bold, be innovative, take risks. Enlarge your concept of "help".
7 Reduce the use made of prison: we endorse ideas such as (Rutherford, *Prisons and the Process of Justice*, 1986):

— reducing the size of the prison system and minimizing its population;
— establishing and enforcing minimum standards within prisons;
— defining staffing ratios qualitatively as well as quantatively; calling people up to serve their sentences to avoid overcrowding;
— having an independent monitor of prisoners' rights;
— reducing lengths of sentences regarded as typical or appropriate;

8 Reduce the size of prison populations, and change the characteristics of institutions:

— build smaller prisons, with smaller units/groupings within them;

— demilitarise them as much as possible;
— ensure that they are resourced to express justice and humanity;
— be more open about them and let the community in to be involved;
— re-introduce effective after-care support.

9 Prisons should have the duties of providing security, order, and safety within their perimeters; of treating inmates with respect, care, and hope; and of having régimes which are positive, fair, and normalised, and which encourage the building of constructive relationships (see Bottoms, *The Aims of Imprisonment.* 1990, p. 17, *et seq*).

10 Extend the availability of community based services — hostels, bail addresses, etc — for use in connection with remand.

11 The use of custodial remand for homelessness, or for those under the influence of various addictions, should be stopped.

12 Those who have to be in custody on remand, of whatever age, should not be in the same institutions as convicted people. The institutions for them should provide "normalised" conditions as a matter of right.

Do not think this can be done on the cheap. The switches of policy we propose will involve spending money rather differently, and on areas that are grossly neglected at present.

It is possible to have a radically different system. There is no compulsion to respond to crime in the way currently operative.

Recommendations to Christians and Churches

1 Practice what you preach. Forgiveness is at the centre of the Gospel message. It is for all — no one is beyond its reach.

2 The church should be the visible expression of forgiveness.

3 Resist any ideas that vengeance and punitiveness should be the main responses of Christians to crime and offending.

4 Ensure that your local congregation/presbytery/church meeting discusses this book. Explore what opportunities you may have locally as a group or as a local church to become practically involved in the penal system.
5 Get the issues of criminal justice policy raised at a national level in your denomination. The churches have great scopeto be direct providers of services for people in trouble.
6 Support the work of chaplains in prisons, and develop links with them to reduce their feeling of isolation from the churches.
7 Speak out, in true prophetic fashion, against injustices where you come across them as you become involved in the criminal justice system.
8 Offer also a message of hope and encouragement to those working in the system who are also battling to reduce injustice and improve conditions. Do not join in the easy condemnation of their efforts and results.
9 We have much to repent of as Christians and churches in our support of injustice, our hesitating witness, and reluctance to take risks.

Recommendations — A Summary

1 Do not make punishment the be all and end all of criminal justice.
2 Replace the familiar association of ideas "crime — punishment" with an alternative pairing, namely "offence — reconciliation".
3 Forgiveness should be the "end" of punishment. This is the ideal which might fill the gap left by the collapse of rehabilitation.
4 The penal system is the not way to solve the problem of crime. It may do quite a lot to exacerbate the problem.
5 Divert some people out of the system altogether — for example, those under 18, those with severe problems of substance abuse, those in great need.
6 Try the use of any scheme which offers alternative ways of sorting out disputes and conflicts without the use of court and punishment.

7 Adopt the aim of "responding justly to offenders". The objectives are to look for ways of creating new relationships and restoring broken ones; to help all parties — victim, offender, society — affected by a crime to find new solutions and outcomes.

8 Reduce the use made of prisons; the size of both the prison populations and the institutions in which they are contained; and the typical lengths of sentences imposed.

9 Replace the emphasis on control, oppression, and isolation with shared responsibility, opportunities for growth, and the goal of re-integration into the community.

10 See criminals as fellow human beings. We are all in much the same condition from the divine perspective. No one is entitled to throw the first stone.

Bibliography

American Friends Service Committee: *Struggle for Justice* (New York: Hill & Wang, 1971).

Association of Directors of Social Work: *Fines and Fine Default* (1987).

Backett, S: "Suicide and Stress in Prison: Implications for a Preventive Strategy in Imprisonment Today" in S Backett, J McNeill and A Yellowless (eds): *Imprisonment Today: Current Issues in the Prison Debate* (Basingstoke: MacMillan, 1988).

Barry, M and R Sidaway: *Help on Release* (CSV Scotland: 1988).

Board for Social Responsibility of the Church of England: *Christians and Delinquency*

Bottoms, A E and R H Preston (eds): *The Coming Penal Crisis* (Scottish Academic Press: 1980)

Bottoms, A E: "Law and Order in Christian Perspective" in *Law and Order; Prospects for the Future* (Centre for Theology and Public Issues: 1986), paper no 10;

Bottoms, A E: "The Aims of Imprisonment" in *Justice, Guilt, and Forgiveness in the Penal System* (Centre for Theology and Public Issues: 1990), paper no 18.

Caird, R: *Good and Useful Life* (Hart-Davis: 1974).

Carlen, Pat: *Women's Imprisonment: A Study in Social Control* (London: RKP, 1983).

Carrel, C (ed), with Joyce Laing, Alice Bain: *The Special Unit Barlinnie Prison: its evolution through its art; an anthology of essays, statements, art works, creative writing, and documentary photographs* (Glasgow: Third Eye Centre, 1982).

Centre for Theology and Public Issues: *Law and Order; Prospects for the Future* (1986), paper no 10.

Centre for Theology and Public Issues: *Justice, Guilt and Forgiveness in the Penal System* (1990), paper no 18.

Colson C (et al): *Crime and the Responsible Community* (Hodder and Stoughton: 1979).

Corbett, C: (see under "Maguire, M" below).

Downes, D: *Contrasts in Tolerance: Post-war Penal Policy in the Netherlands and England and Wales* (OUP: 1988).

Duff, A: "Punishment, Repentance and Forgiveness" in *Justice, Guilt, and Forgiveness in the Penal System* (Centre for Theology and Public Issues: 1990), paper no 18.

Fabian Society: *Conviction Politics: A Plan for Penal Policy* (1987).

Forrester, D B and D Skene (eds): *Just Sharing: A Christian Approach to the Distribution of Wealth Income and Benefits* (Epworth: 1988).

Forum for Initiatives in Reparation and Mediation: *FIRM News* and *Mediation* (1989), various issues.

Fox, L: *The English Prison and Borstal System* (RKP: 1952).

Hardy, Right Revd R, Bishop of Lincoln: "The Meaning of Imprisonment' (1989), transcript of conference.

Haxby, D: *Probation, a Changing Service* (London: Constable, 1978).

HM Institution, Cornton Vale: "Female Behaviour" (1982).

HMSO: *Report of the Inquiry into the United Kingdom Prison Services* (The May Report: 1979), Cmnd 7673.

HMSO: *Keeping Offenders Out of Court; Further Alternatives to Prosecution* (The Stewart Committee Second Report: 1983).

HMSO: *Report of the Review of suicide precautions at Glenochil* (The Chiswick Report: 1985).

HMSO: *Parole and Related Issues in Scotland* (Report of the Kincraig Committee: 1988), Cmnd 598.

Hodgson Committee (1984): *Profits of Crime and their Recovery* (London: Heinemann).

Home Office: *The Sentence of the Court* (1986).

Home Office: *Punishment, Custody and the Community* (1988).

Home Office: *Bringing People Together: Mediation and Reparation Projects in Great Britain* (Marshall and Walpole Research and Planning Unit: 1985), paper no 33.

Home Office: *A Preliminary Study of Victim Offender Mediation and Reparation Schemes in England and Wales* (Research and Planning Unit Paper), no 42.

Home Office: *Partnership in Dealing with Offenders in the Community* (1990).

Hough, M and P Mayhew: *Taking Account of Crime: Key Findings of the Second British Crime Survey* (Home Office Research Study), no 85 (London: HMSO, 1985).

Hoyles, F: *Punishment in the Bible* (1986).

Howard League for Scotland: *Helping Out—Towards Alternatives to Imprisonment* (1985).

Howard League for Scotland: *Probation—A Suitable Case for Treatment* (1987).

Inter-Church Working Party/Prison Chaplaincy Board of the Church of Scotland: "The Work of Chaplains" (1988).

Irish Council for Social Welfare: "The Prison System" (Dublin: 1983, reprinted 1986).

Irish Council of Churches and the Commission for Justice and Peace: "Human Rights, Social Justice, Development" (Dublin: 1986).

Irish Council of Churches and the Commission for Justice and Peace: "Punishment and Imprisonment" (Dublin: Dominican Publications, 1985).

Irish Council of Churches and the Commission for Justice and Peace: "Response to the Report of the Committee of Inquiry into the Penal System" (1986).

Jenkins, Right Revd D, Bishop of Durham: "The Meaning of Imprisonment" (1989), transcript of conference.

Joint Review Group on Services to Offenders Report: a group of officers from Social Work Services Group and the Association of Directors of Social Work in Scotland (1985), unpublished.

King, J: *The Probation Service* (Butterworth: 1969).

King, R and R Morgan: *The Future of the Prison System* (1980).

Kinsey, R: "Crisis? Whose Crisis?" in *Law and Order: Prospects for the Future* (Centre for Theology and Public Issues: 1986), paper no 10.

Knapper, P: "The Development of Mediation Schemes in France, 1983-1987" in *Crucible* (April-June 1988).

Laing, J: (see under "Carrel, C" above).

Lothian Regional Department of Social Work: "Probation Contract".

Lothian Regional Department of Social Work: *Newsletter on Working With Offenders*, various issues.

Lothian Regional Department of Social Work: "The Edinburgh Social Work Diversion Scheme", first two reports.

MacKintosh, H R: *The Christian Experience of Forgiveness* (Fontana: 1961).

MacKay, R E: *Reparation in Criminal Justice* (SACRO: 1988).

MacKinnon, A: forthcoming work in Christian Ethics and Criminal Justice (Edinburgh: 1990).

Mathiesen, T: *Prison on Trial* (New York: Sage, 1990).

Maguire, M and Corbett, C: *The Effects of Crime and the Work of the Victims Support Schemes* (Cambridge Studies in Criminology: 1987), LVI.

Maguire, M (ed) and J Pointing: *Victims of Crime: A New Deal* (Open University Press: 1988).

Moore, G and C Wood: *Social Work and Criminal Law in Scotland* (Aberdeen University Press: 1981, updated 1985).

Moore, G: *A Guide to the Children's Hearings* (Green & Son: 1989).

Morris, T: "Consensus Versus Ideology—Problems for Contemporary Penal Policy" in *Justice, Guilt and Forgiveness in the Penal System* (Centre for Theology and Public Issues: 1990), paper no 18.

National Association for the Care and Resettlement of Offenders: "Prisons and Penal Policy" (1988).

National Association for the Care and Resettlement of Offenders: "Remands in Custody" (Briefing Paper), no 32; "Criteria for Custody" (Briefing Paper), no 69; "Disturbances in Prison Establishments" (Briefing Paper), no 97.

National Association of Probation Officers: "Probation, A Case for Growth" (1983).

Nicholson, Sheriff C G B: *The Law and Practice of Sentencing in Scotland* (Green: 1981).

Nicholson, Sheriff C G B: "Sentencing Policy and the Failure of Rehabilitation" in *Law and Order; Prospects for the Future* (Centre for Theology and Public Issues: 1986), paper no 10.

The Observer Magazine: "Guilt" (4.12.88).

Observer Review: "Behind Bars" (13.11.88); "No Way Out" (27.11.88).

Pointing J: (see under "Maguire, M" above).

Preston, R H: "The Justice Model and Forgiveness" in *Justice, Guilt and Forgiveness in the Penal System* (Centre for Theology and Public Issues: 1990), paper no 18. See also "Bottoms, A E and R H Preston" above.

Prisons (Scotland) Act, 1952 and Prison Rules (HMSO).

Rifkind, M: "Kenneth Younger Memorial Lecture" (Howard League for Scotland: 1988).

Rutherford, A: *Prisons and the Process of Justice* (OUP: 1986).

The Scotsman Newspaper: "How to Make Punishment fit the crime" (23.5.88); "Inside Dealing in Hope" (24.8.88); "Fresh Start—Fresh Problems: do we need jail so many?" (13.10.88); "Turning Away from the Monuments to the past" (24.4.90).

Scottish Convention of Women: "Submission to the Kincraig Committee (on Parole)".

Scottish Health Education Group: "Families Visiting Scottish Prisons" (1989), information sheet.

Scottish Home and Health Department: Parole and Related Issues in Scotland; the government's response to the report of the review committee (1989).

Scottish Prison Service and Social Work Services Group: *Continuity through cooperation: a national framework of policy and practice guidance for social work in Scottish Penal establishments* (1989).

Scottish Prison Service: *Assessment and Control: the management of violent and disruptive prisoners* (1988).

Scottish Prison Service: *Business Plan* (1989-1992).

Scottish Prison Service: *Current Issues in Scottish Prisons: systems of accountability and régimes for difficult prisoners* (1989).

Scottish Prison Service: *Custody and Care: policy and plans for the Scottish Prison Service* (1988).

Scottish Prison Service: *Opportunity and Responsibility: developing new approaches to the management of long term prison system in Scotland* (1990).

Scottish Prison Service: *Social Work in Prison: a challenging task in a changing environment* (1989).

Shapland, J with Jon Willmore and Peter Duff: *Victims in the criminal justice system* (Cambridge Studies in Criminology), LIII (Gower Publishing: 1985).

Shaw, R: *Children of imprisoned Fathers* (Hodder and Stoughton: 1987).

Speller, A: *Breaking Out: a Christian Critique of Criminal Justice* (British Council of Churches: 1986).

Stern, V: *Bricks of Shame: Britain's Prisons* (Penguin Special: 1987).

Thomson, A: "Has the Prison system failed?" in *Law and Order; Prospects for the Future* (Centre for Theology and Public Issues: 1986), paper no 10.

Times Newspaper: "Crusade against sociological alibis of criminals" (23.3.88); "Punishment in a Caring Society" (24.10.88).

Walkyate, S: *Victimology: the victim and the criminal justice process* (Unwin and Hyman: 1989).

Wilde, O: quoted in L Fox: *The English Prison and Borstal System* (1952).

Wood, C: *The Social Worker's guide to reports for criminal courts* (Lothian Region Social Work Department).

Wood, C: (see under "Moore, G" above).